I'm Changing The Game

Lessons From The Playbook Of Philippians

Dr. John R. Adolph

Table Of Contents

About The Author

Dr. John R. Adolph

Dr. John R. Adolph is a called servant of God and one of the greatest voices in the body of Christ for this generation. He is the Senior Pastor of Antioch Missionary Baptist Church in Beaumont, Texas. He often serves as an evangelist for revivals and crusades; he is an author, a sought-after conference speaker, and well-established community leader.

Dr. Adolph is a proud graduate of M. B. Smiley Senior High School in Houston, Texas earning his diploma; Texas Southern University earning his B.B.A. with a concentration in Finance and Accounting; the Interdenominational Theological Center, Morehouse School of Religion earning his MDIV with a concentration in Pastoral Care and Counseling; Houston Graduate School of Theology with a Doctor of Ministry Degree; and the Oxford Round Table, Oxford, England.

Dr. Adolph serves as the President of Exalting the Savior Ministries, LLC, a nationally recognized organization that seeks to empower the people of God spiritually, economically, socially, relationally, and physically. He currently streams to a waiting web-based congregation of thousands and preaches to millions via IMPAC Broadcasting Network and TBN Broadcasting Network in Jefferson County, Texas.

Dr. Adolph has authored several books to include *Victorious Christian Living, Vol. 1 & 2, Let Me Encourage You, I'm Coming Out of This; Marriage is for Losers and Celibacy is for Fools.* Dr. Adolph serves on the Board of Trustees of Baptist Hospital, the I Have A Dream Program of Beaumont, Texas, as the President of Jehovah Jireh Village, and on the Board of Directors for the National Baptist Convention, USA, Inc.

He has faithfully served at Antioch for 18 years and has seen the Lord grow the congregation from 250 to a faith-fellowship of well over 9,000. The current ministry campus consists of over 120,000 square feet of plant and facility, a beautiful neighborhood called Jehovah Jireh Village I & II; a townhouse development called Grace Lakes, which is now home to over 140 residents; and is currently working to implement an academic institution for children called the Royal Ambassador Academy.

Dr. Adolph is married to the love of his life Dorrie Eileen, and is the proud father of two great kids, Sumone Elizabeth and Jonathan Raeshawn.

Victory
Is Your Destiny

You're about to embark upon a 40-day journey of excitement! For the next six weeks, you will be sharing God's Word with those who are in your group and/or class. Of course, you could do this study alone, but this study will come out greater if you share it with family, friends and people you love. With this in mind, once a week gather with the people who make up your group. Design a set place and time for you to meet. Each group session should last no more than an hour and a half. You should have a DVD that contains inspirational messages from Dr. Adolph (if you're not the group leader, your leader should have the disc) and a workbook in hand that consists of group sessions designed to enrich you and individual devotionals composed to inspire you. Start each group session by following the directions given at the start of each chapter. When the group sessions have been concluded there will be time allotted for dialogue and discussion concerning lesson.

During the week, you will need to carve out of your busy schedule at least seven minutes a day for God. This will be your devotional time. This can happen at any point in your day, but make it happen at the same time every day no matter what. During this seven-minute period, you will read the letter of Philippians and write some of your thoughts in your journal. You will find this time of journaling each day both healing and refreshing.

With this in mind, never forget that the Bible is the greatest book that history will ever have in its possession. It is God breathed, spiritually dictated, and divinely inspired. It is a portion of the mind of God on paper; it is bread for the hungry, a light for those in darkness, healing for the wounded, strength for the weak, direction for the lost, a constitution for those who are a part of God's Kingdom on earth and a road map to victory for every believer who will live its principles and practice its precepts. Therefore, a crucial key to victory in your destiny is to feed your soul God's Word daily.

Your life is about to change for the better! As you study God's Word over the next few weeks, you are going to encounter Jesus Christ in some wonderful ways. You will see that in sin, He is a Savior; in darkness, He is a light; in confusion, He is direction; in bondage, He is a liberator; in sickness, He is a physician; in times of hurt, He is a healer; in loneliness, He is a steadfast companion; in weakness, He is your strength; in death, He is your life; and in life, He is your victory. Jesus Christ is our victorious, vicarious King! The finished work of the Lord Jesus Christ at Calvary sealed the scoreboard of life with a win against sin and satan for us once and for all.

Victory is your destiny!

But thanks be to God, which giveth us victory through our Lord Jesus Christ.
I Corinthians 15:57

WEEK 1

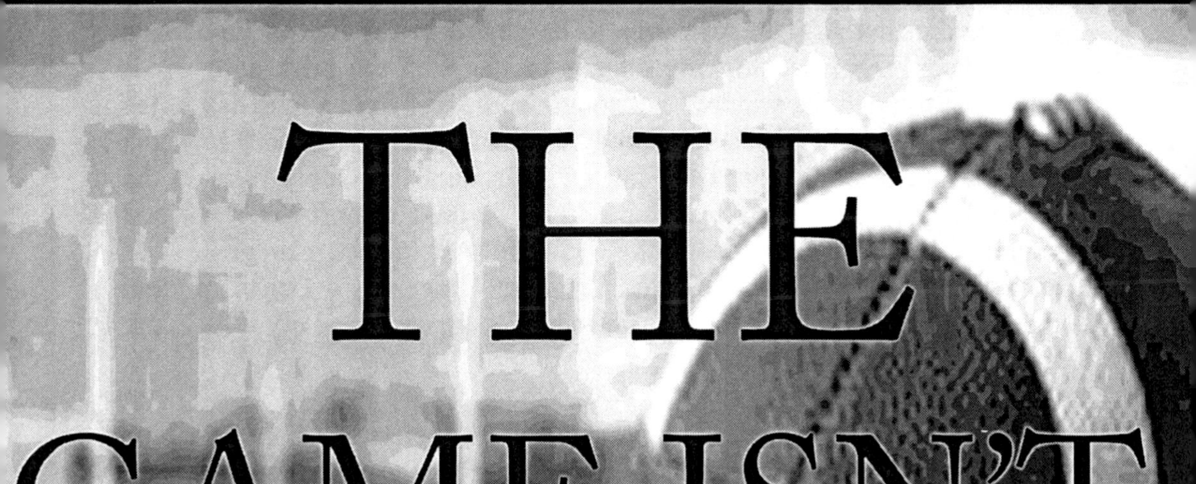

THE GAME ISN'T OVER YET

Paul and Timotheus, the servants of Jesus Christ, to all the saints in Christ Jesus which are at Philippi, with the bishops and deacons: Grace be unto you, and peace, from God our Father, and from the Lord Jesus Christ (Philippians 1:1-2).

While in London, I picked up a USA Today and noticed that Warren Moon, famed quarterback from the Houston Oilers in Houston, Texas, became the first African American to be placed in the Hall of Fame as a quarterback. As I sat thinking on this matter with the brisk cool winds whipping through the window as I sought some rest from a long day in the UK, it hit me. I quickly remembered the first time I had a chance to watch him play in person. It was the fall of 1985, and the Oilers were in the playoffs. They were matched and heavily favored against the weak and fragile Cincinnati Bengals in the Houston Astrodome. The game was supposed to be a blowout. Texas Southern University's Ocean of Soul marching band was there to perform at half-time, and I had my tuba in my hand.

The stadium was packed. The atmosphere was electric. Canadian blue and white were everywhere. The cheerleaders were cheering; fans were screaming, and it was time to get the party started! However, somebody forgot to tell Cincinnati that they were supposed to lose. They won the coin toss and elected to receive. The kickoff went well until a young man caught the ball on his three-yard line and ran it all the way back for a touchdown......7-0 in favor of Cincinnati. Okay, that was luck, right? Warren Moon takes the field, and his first pass is picked off and returned for another touchdown.........14-0 Cincinnati. A hush fell over the crowd. The Bengals get the ball and drive it all the way down the field, eating up the clock, making the Oilers look like a dysfunctional college team with a bad coach and a sorry playbook........21-0 in favor of Cincinnati. And, then just before the end of the second quarter one of the oldest plays in the book, a flea flicker that works. We go in at the half 28-0. People were disgusted. Cheerleaders had an attitude as if to say, "I put on all of this make-up for nothing!" And, we were getting ready to come down out of the stands to perform.

It was at that time that I heard it. A middle-aged woman seated next to a man who appeared to be semi-inebriated said to him, "Honey the team is leaving the field, and the game is over! Let's go. This was a waste of money and a waste of time!" The man standing there with a beer in his hand and already one too many in his system responded in this fashion, "Woman don't be crazy! Our team is just getting warmed up! They just wanted to see what the Bengals had to throw at them that is all! Bum Phillips is about to change his game plan, and things are about to get good! Oh, no we're not leaving; it's only half-time, and the game isn't over yet!"

People have it bad. We have a habit of writing people off when things don't look like they are going to work out. Has it ever happened to you before? Where your current condition did not look so hot, and there were those near you that wrote you off before the game was over? If this has happened to you, just know that you are not alone. However, I believe that the overwhelming contention made throughout this letter is simple yet profound. Here is the one thing that is made clear, never ever let your current condition today determine what your tomorrow looks like. God has a habit of turning things around! Here's the announcement of joy, strength and power that comes from this wonderful letter to the people of God who love the Lord Jesus Christ, "The game isn't over yet!"

Here he is again; that great Apostle born out of due season, our gospel globetrotter the Apostle Paul and his sidekick from Lystra whose name is Timothy. Paul is writing to a small group of faithful believers located in a Roman colony, which bears the name Philippi. From the outside in, the game looks bleak. The aged Apostle is locked up in a Neronian jail awaiting his trial and probable execution. There are those who are talking negatively about him, hoping to add affliction to his bonds and there are others who love him, but are on the timid side. It appears that Paul is out for the season, and so is this newly formulated religious sect called Christians. Here's the mistake they made, they let Paul run off the field and get a chalkboard in his hand and something to write with, and he comes out with a game plan that is mind blowing for this young Philippian team.

He comes out with a playbook whose watchword is joy! He opens the letter by gathering his team around him at the half to give them instructions. He says Epaphroditus is back on his feet, and Timothy is ready to go. Our adversaries think that the game is over, but it's just half-time and the victory is ours. Put your hands in and shout victory on three! One, two, three…victory! The huddle breaks and the letter commences!

This book is designed to be an exciting contemporary journey through the Epistle of Philippians for those who want to change the game. This chapter is for people who have had a rough time and have had others write you off. This missive is for the student, who is headed back to school, and you had a tough year last year and some people think this year will be a repeat of last year. This work is for the administrator who was treated unfairly, and your peers think that your career is over. This text is for a couple whose marriage is struggling, and it is starting to seem as if all is lost. This communiqué is for the saint who is physically ill, and the prognosis of your situation looks bleak. This chapter is for the believer who has suffered a death in the family, and you feel like you just cannot go on. And, these pages have been written for the seasoned saint whose skin is wrinkled, and some people think that because you are older, you are washed up. Here's the great news of this letter. Here's the news that brings healing and wholeness. The game isn't over yet! It's time for you to rethink your victory, revisit your purpose and come out with your head up and ready to move forward!

I know, you are saying all of this sounds great, but what should I do to turn things around in my life? This is the core study of this chapter. Paul makes it clear that if you are going to turn things around there are some things that are a must in order to cause it to come to fruition.

Week One

THE GROUP ENCOUNTER

Let's Get Started

1. Take this moment to introduce yourself to everyone in your group.
2. Share an experience that you have had in your life that made you feel like "the game was over."
3. Discuss how you made it through that season of your life.

A Look At The Playbook

Watch DVD for "Group Encounter 1" and complete the section below.

A_____who is saved.

Most of the people you think are real authentic friends in your
_____aren't.

Paul is in jail, and that is when _____ shows up.
Now that's a real friend and a friend indeed.

They are both _____ of Christ Jesus. The
Greek word for "servant" is "duolos." It means to be a slave, but check
this out. It means to be a slave even after you have been freed.

I have always been taught that the company that we keep will always
define us. If we run with wolves, we will learn to _____.

A _____ that is saturated.

If you are changing the game in your life, an ordinary
_____ fellowship will not do.

When saints live right, bishops oversee the flock with integrity and deacons serve with a sense of passion and purpose, the person of the _____ moves through the church, and awesome things happen.

A fuel that _____.

Here's the truth, all of us run low from time to time and need a _____.

Grace (charis) deals with God's unmerited _____ He shows towards you and _____(iraynay) deals with God's presence that flows from you.

A _____that's solid.

Now is not the time for new ideas and gimmicks; stick to what _____.

God our _____ and Jesus Christ, His _____

Jesus put it like this, even when you look like you are losing the _____, He says "and lo I am with you always even till the end of the earth!"

The Locker Room Chat

Take a moment to dialogue and discuss as a group the video presentation using the questions below to lead the conversation.

1. Believers will never grow into strong disciples in the Lord without good friends in the faith. In what ways have friends in the Christian faith helped you grow and develop as a believer?
2. Every believer needs to be involved with the Lord's Church (Hebrews 10:25). In what ways do you gain strength from your church fellowship?

3. There are some of you who know that your game should be over. But God has given you more grace and granted you unusual favor. What are you doing with the life God has extended towards you right now?
4. Paul uses the word "servant" to describe himself in relation to Jesus Christ. He clearly stated that he was a "servant" of the Lord. If you are truly a servant, where do you serve? In what ways can you serve God more?
5. You've still got some game left. You're alive, and that means that God is not through with you yet. Discuss one major change that you need to make in your life, one that you are not going to wait to change. You are ready to start right now.

It's Game Time

Prayer Assignment: Commit to a designated prayer time each day. Let nothing stop you from prayer time with the Lord. Find a place that you will designate as your prayer ground and for the next six weeks meet God there every day. This does not have to be a fancy place. You can meet the Lord at your bedside, your kitchen table, your desk at work, etc. No matter where you meet God, the place should remain the same each day.

Reading Assignment: Read Philippians 1 in its entirety before the next group session.

Memory Verse: Phil. 1:6-Being confident of this very thing, that He which hath begun a good work in you will perform it until the day of Jesus Christ.

Day 1

Not Arrogant, But Confident!

One of the greatest athletes of all time is Muhammad Ali. He was a skillful boxer who faced defeat, but knew well the sweet taste of victory. On one particular occasion, while being interviewed by famed ABC sports anchorman Howard Cosell, he was asked why he was so arrogant. Ali's response shocked the nation. He said, "Howard, there's a difference between being arrogant and being confident! I'm confident, and my confidence makes people like you uncomfortable. And yeah I brag a lot, but it ain't bragging if it's true."

Ali was confident in what he could produce in the ring as a boxer. Likewise, we as Christians should be confident in what God produces in our lives by faith as believers.

Are you confident in the Lord?

Read Philippians 1:3-7

Paul describes himself as "confident" in verse 6. What has God done in your life that has made you confident in Him?

There are times in the life of every believer that you can feel defeated because some of your old habits that you just knew were dead and gone surface again. Has this ever happened to you? If so, do you believe that God is going to complete the work that He started in your life?

No Christian is perfect. We are all flawed; however, the Lord is perfecting us and changing us each day into the image of His Son. In what ways can you say that God has changed you?

Look inwardly and sincerely at your life for a moment. Make a personal list of things that you would like to see God change in you so that you can change the game in your life.

Read 2 Corinthians 5:17

What do these words say to you? What confidence do they place in your heart?

Daily Prayer:

Lord, cause me to be confident in the salvation that you have given me through your only-begotten Son, Jesus Christ. Draw me closer to you, mold me with your hands, fill me with your spirit and order my steps according to your Word. I pray this prayer in the name of Jesus Christ, Amen.

Your Journal
Prayers, Thoughts & Notes:

Day 2

Teamwork Makes The Dream Work!

One player can be a difference maker or even a game changer, but no one man can win a championship by himself. It takes a team. One of the greatest teams in sports history was the Chicago Bulls during the era of head coach Phil Jackson. The Bulls were a dynasty with players on the team like Michael Jordan, Scottie Pippin, Dennis Rodman, Steve Kerr and the list goes on. These were men who knew how to win, and they won it. In fact, they won it all six times! Today they still hold the record for most championships gained by a single team in one sport. What made them win was not just the talent of Jordan or the shooting ability of Kurr. It was not the rebounding ability of Rodman or even the toughness of Pippin. They won because they played as a team.

As a believer in Jesus Christ, we need each other to help victory come to pass. Teamwork really does make the dream work.

What people help you run the Christian race? Who's on your team?

Read Philippians 1:7-11

It is clear that Paul loved the believers who were in Philippi and counted them to be people he shared the faith of the Lord with as friends. Who are some of your friends in the faith?

In strength training, it is imperative to have a spotter present. That's the person who helps you to push the weight off of you when you are too weak to push it for yourself. Spotters make us strong. Who are some people who work with you as a Christian who make you stronger?

What do they do for you that make you a better believer in the Lord?

Read St. John 13:34, 1 John 2:7-8 and 2 John 5

It is clear from these verses that God wants people on His team to love each other. In what ways has this been easy for you?

In what ways has this been extremely difficult for you?

The enemy's plan is to keep you at odds with other believers so that you grow weaker and not stronger. Write out a plan that will keep you connected to strong believers while enduring an attack from the enemy.

Daily Prayer:

God, keep me near believers who are near you and love you. Please move people away from me who seek to pull me away from you. Bless the relationships that I am involved in so that the people who are in my nearby circle of influence would love one another as we love you. Hear my prayer O God, in the name of Jesus Christ, I petition you, Amen.

Your Journal
Prayers, Thoughts & Notes:

Day 3

I May Be Down, But Don't Count Me Out!

On February 11, 1990, James "Buster" Douglas shocked the world. He gained enough courage to step into the boxing ring with the most ferocious boxer known in the industry; the WBA/WBC undefeated undisputed heavyweight champion of the world, Iron Mike Tyson. For all practical purposes, this fight was supposed to be an easy purse and a nice sparring match for the champion. After all, Tyson was 37-0 and Douglas was an unheard of boxer with several wins over opponents with questionable skills. As the fight enters the eighth round, Tyson drops Douglas to the canvas. It appeared that the champion had defeated yet another foe. But, someone forgot to tell Douglas he was supposed to lose. He rose from the canvas and went on to defeat Mike Tyson in round 10, not just beating the champion, but knocking him out!

Here's the cold hard truth about being a believer in Jesus Christ, there are times when life will drop you to the canvas. It is then that you must make a decision that to be knocked down does not mean that you are knocked out.

Rise to your feet and keep on fighting onward to victory.

Read Philippians 1:12-18

The letter of Philippians is called a "prison letter or epistle." The reason for this is because while this letter is being written the Apostle Paul is a prisoner in Rome with Nero on the throne. In short, he is down, but he is not out.

Life can hit all of us from time to time and knock us down. How has your being hit matured you in the faith?

Often the only Bible that unbelievers will ever see or read is the one they see you live each day. How has your ability to suffer and still believe in the Lord helped others who are near you?

One of the toughest questions believers often ask is "why does God let bad things happen to good people?" What if God wanted to use your life as an example so that others might see how He sustains you during a time of difficulty? How would you feel? What would you do?

Read Job 1 & Job 42:10

There's no doubt that Job was down, but the blessing of his testimony is that he was not out. How do you feel about your life's story? If you could write a book what would be the title? Have you ever thought about writing your story for others to gain strength from it?

Daily Prayer:

Lord of heaven, there have been moments in my journey when life has knocked me to the canvas. But, you have always been my strength and my joy. Use my life with all of its ups and downs to win others to you as did the Apostle Paul. Thank you for being my way up when I was knocked out. In the name of the Lord of Heaven, I pray, Amen.

Your Journal
Prayers, Thoughts & Notes:

Day 4

Losing Is Not An Option!

He was born in Towson, Maryland where he learned to swim, and the rest is history. It doesn't matter whether it is the backstroke, butterfly, freestyle or an individual medley, he is a winner. In the 2008 summer Olympic Games in Beijing, he dominated his opponents by bringing eight gold medals to the United States of America. In short, Michael "The Baltimore Bullet" Phelps was made to swim. At present, Phelps holds the record for the most medals ever won in both national and international games. He holds fifty-eight gold medals, eleven silver medals and three bronze medals. In a recent blog article that boasted his stats and his illustrious career, the title of the article said it all. The core, crux and center regarding the victories of Michael Phelps simply bear this mantra "losing is not an option!"

Defeat may come and go from time to time, but losing is never a good option unless you win in the end!

Read Philippians 1:19-20

As Paul writes to the Philippian Church, he presses upon them the importance of prayer, the person of the Holy Spirit and the hope of all believers. Rate your personal prayer life and be honest.

Excellent   _____
Good   _____
Average   _____
Below Average _____
Needs Help   _____

Prayer is the key to spiritual victory on every front. It is a spiritual exercise that always yields results that are supernatural and cannot be seen with the naked eye. Use your imagination and describe what you think happens in the throne room of God when you start to pray.

There are times Christians are ridiculed for praying in public. Has this ever happened to you? What happened that day? How did it make you feel?

Daily prayer requires a place that you meet God. Here's a devotional question for you to ponder, where do you go to meet God and share with Him intimately? If you do not have a prayer place, it could be because you're not spending enough time in prayer. Use this devotional moment to go and mark a place where you plan to meet God each day.

What if you found out that God wanted to spend more time with you, what would you do? If so, why not start meeting and sharing with Him today.

Read St. Matthew 5:5-8

When Jesus gives you the promise of answered prayer how does it make you feel?

Daily Prayer:

Lord, my soul, is thirsty for you. Forgive me for not spending more time with you. Today I plan to change that starting right now. I love you, and I know that you love me. I know that losing is not an option for me because I am winning in you every single moment of the day. Jesus you are my victory and I am not a victim; I am a vicarious victor who wins against all odds. In Christ's name, Amen!

Your Journal
Prayers, Thoughts & Notes:

Day 5

For The Love Of The Game!

February 18, 2001 is a day that NASCAR fans will never forget. It's the Daytona 500 and cars were in their last lap when all of a sudden car #36 kissed car #3 carrying one of the greatest drivers of all time. His name was Dale Earnhardt. At first glance, the accident did not seem life threatening, after all, Earnhardt had been involved in numerous accidents over the course of his career. But, this time the angle in which his car struck the wall, traveling at a speed of nearly 150 miles per hour, proved to be fatal. During the time, the nation and millions of fans mourned his death; ESPN did a special tribute to him and his accomplishments on the track. During the tribute, they showed Earnhardt leaving a burning vehicle where it appeared that he would never race again because the sport had proven to be very dangerous, and he knew that he could perish. But Earnhardt would hear no such thing. He continued racing not because he needed the money, not for the fame or for the celebrity endorsements. He did it because he loved the game.

Like a game, life for the believer in Jesus Christ is to be lived not because we have the best of conditions or because we possess the best of circumstances, but purely because we love the Lord and we love the game.

Read Philippians 1:21-24

Paul is not a fair-weather believer. He is in it with Jesus Christ, win, lose or draw. After reading the verses listed above, how do you feel about Paul's faith in God?

Imagine several gunmen walking into a crowded church cathedral on a Sunday while the congregation is singing "O How I Love Jesus" when they fire several warning shots into the air. After the shots are fired, and the music stops, they say to those who are present, "Everyone who loves Jesus Christ will die today. Everyone else who is just present for the service may leave in peace." Now imagine preachers leaving, deacons walking out and the pews emptying as fast as they filled. Would you be in the crowd that leaves? Would you stay? Be real with your answer.

We live in the era of the fair-weather believer. We are not big on commitments, covenants and lasting relationships. With this in mind, ponder some things you would die to save or stand for.

Now be honest, was Jesus Christ on your list? Why or why not?

Read St. John 3:16

If Jesus Christ loved you enough to die so that you could live, He wants a Christian who will return that same love in commitment to Him and live for Him until he or she dies. With this in mind, look earnestly at your life and make a decision today that you're going to live and die for the cause of Jesus Christ.

Daily Prayer:

Lord, my faith in you and your finished work on the cross, is worth dying for. I have made up my mind that living for you each moment causes me to die to self so that I can live in you. God, I have no life to live without you. Lord Jesus, it is in you that I live, move and exist. Use my life to bring you glory until the day that I die. In Jesus name, Amen!

Your Journal
Prayers, Thoughts & Notes:

WEEK 2

'M IN IT
TO
WIN IT!

And having this confidence, I know that I shall continue with you all for your furtherance and joy in the faith; that your rejoicing may be more abundant in Jesus Christ for me by my coming to you again (Phil. 1:24-25).

It is September 16, 2013, and 57-year-old Bill Nye is preparing to go to battle. Nye is the famed PBS Science guy who wears a bow tie as he helps kids across the country grapple with the intricacies of matter and human existence. His battle this time is not in a lab with a test tube in his hand, it is on Dancing with the Stars. He's set to do the tango, but there are several problems that he has to face. His opponents are at least ten years younger than he is and to make matters worse, rhythm is not one of his greatest assets. Nye interviewed with CBS News reporter Jessica Derschowitz, and openly admitted that the odds were stacked against him and that he was nervous about the whole "dancing" thing. In fact, he admits to being completely terrified. After all, Bill is a science man, not a guy who is made for the dance floor. But he is determined not just to compete, but to win the whole thing. When asked about his thought regarding his chances, Bill Nye replied in this fashion, "I've come too far to turn around now! I'm in it, to win it!"

I rejoiced and shouted when I heard this expression. "I'm in it, to win it!" What a concept. Here's the truth and take it for what it is worth to you, all of us have faced some moments in life when the odds were stacked against us. For some people, the odds have been stacked against you financially. Poverty is something that seems like it may not ever change in your life. For others, it is physical infirmity, and still for others it is family challenges. But, why live in defeat when the Lord of heaven died so that you might have victory in every facet of your life! Make this your personal mantra for the rest of your life, "I'm in it, to win it!"

Consider this session to be your personal appointment to reassess your life. God is going to take His Word and heal you with it this week. Get ready for a move of God that would bring liberty, peace, healing and deliverance! Can I tell you why you are sharing this moment with me right now? God wants you to know that even though you are in it, you are going to win it.

Here in the passage, Paul is locked up in prison. It is a known fact of the historical-critical method of canonical study that this is one of Paul's prison epistles. He has given us the report that some are trying to hurt him, but the more they try, the more God blesses him. He tells the church that he is caught between two ideas. He wants to go home and be with the Lord, and he desires to stay around and continue sharing the gospel message. It is in this verse that he makes a decision that comes from the heart of the Lord! In layman's terms, what Paul says is, "Yes, I'm on lockdown right now. I am under house arrest, but my current condition does not dictate or define my future position. I do not care about Nero. I do not care about the Praetorian Guard or the numbers of haters trying to hurt me. I am locked up, but I am confident of this thing: I know that I shall abide and continue with you all for your furtherance and joy in the faith that your rejoicing may be more abundant in Jesus Christ for me by my coming to you again!"

Can you feel his passion? Get this, he is locked up, but he says I am coming to you again! His head is on the chopping block, and things look grim, yet he says I am coming to you again! Okay let me give you a retranslation of this verse my way. The great Apostle is declaring, "Where I am now is not where I am going to end up. I have issues with bondage right now but trust me, "I'm in it, to win it!"

In this session, I want to share with some people who are real in the struggle. I want to talk to some people who know if they could just get themselves right things would be better, but you can't do it, so you haven't done it. I want to talk to some people who, after looking carefully at themselves can say, "Yes Lord, I love you, but I have some issues." I want to help some people who have been hurt and struggle to forgive. Today is your day! Declare this with your mouth as you read it, "I'm in it, to win it!" I want to help the saint who is thinking about throwing in the towel on your marriage. Say this to yourself with confidence, "I'm in it, to win it!" I want to offer healing to the man who struggles with promiscuity, help to the woman who has been bound and tied by lesbianism, and freedom to the teen who has lowered their moral standards to live in sin just to fit in. Declare this from your soul as you share this session. Say it in faith, no matter what's behind me, the best part of my life is ahead of me and "I'm it, to win it!!"

I want to give strength to the married believer whose marriage is on the rocks, and you are starting to feel like divorce is a good option. I want to give light to the single saint who is starting to settle for just anybody because you feel like your biological clock is going off. I want to offer blessing to the person who truly tithes and gives but struggles every week financially, and you have been wondering when your harvest is going to come in. I want to offer good news to a child of God, who has been attacked with illness, and you know that your healing is coming, but nobody seems to know when. Say this with passion, "I'm in it, to win it!" I want to offer liberation to the believer who worries too much, freedom to the saint who is constantly filled with anxiety and stress, and emancipation to the new convert who is still trapped in some private sins that you need to come out of. Declare it once more with your mouth. Say it in total belief, "I'm in it, to win it!"

There are several principles that we can gain from just two verses of Paul's teachings that if practiced, will surely help you not just say, "I'm in it, to win it" but live the words that you have been declaring.

Week Two

THE GROUP ENCOUNTER

Let's Get Started

1. Take this moment to introduce yourself to everyone in your group if you have some new people in your group this week.
2. Share an experience that you have had in which the odds were seriously stacked against you.
3. Discuss some of the errors that you made when the odds were against you.
4. If you were in it, but came out of it, discuss with your group how you made it.
5. Describe at least one thing in your life that you got yourself into that God got you out of.

A Look At The Playbook

Watch DVD for "Group Encounter 2" and complete the section below.

Be confident in the _____.

The word choice here is the term "pi-tho." It means to be totally _____. To know without a doubt.

Please internalize this; it is easy to lose confidence in human kind. People tend to _____like the weather.

It is easy to lose confidence in systems. They are made and designed by people who are _____.

It is easy to lose confidence in surgeons and scientists. They are human and they often make _____.

It is easy to lose confidence in _____. There are some things that it will never buy.

But it is hard to lose confidence in _____. For God knows all, sees all, controls all, possesses all and is always there!

Be convinced in the _____ and verbal with the _____.

If you really want to see God move mightily in your life, you are going to have to change what comes out of your _____.

Paul says "…I know that I shall _____ and continue with you all for your furtherance and joy of faith."

If you are going to possess it, you must first _____ it.

This is not a name it and claim it deal. However, it is a matter of _____ and _____ harmony.

Be constant in your _____.

Paul states in the verse, "…..that your rejoicing may be more abundant." The word "_____" is "kow-ka-mah." It refers to the outward expression of a saint that is in direct connection with their inward joy.

In short, it means to express joy with the _____. It means to boast and give glory with the mouth.

The Locker Room Chat

Take a moment to dialogue and discuss as a group the video presentation using the questions below to lead the conversation.

1. There are times when we are in situations that literally shake our faith in God. Have you ever been there before? If so, what happened?

2. There are times when negative thoughts cross our minds, and if we are not careful, those same thoughts fall from our lips. What are some negative thoughts or statements that you have made that you have seen come to life? Discuss this with your group.
3. Paul is fond of the term "know" as we have discussed in this lesson. What are some things that you "know" about the Lord? How do you "know" them?
4. Rejoicing means to boast or brag about something with the mouth. What do you find yourself boasting about mostly? Be honest. How often do you take the time to rejoice in the person of Jesus Christ?
5. If you are in it to win it, it is because you are not in it alone. What role has the Lord played in your life to empower you to win in while you were in it?

It's Game Time

Prayer Assignment: For the next seven days, regardless of your conditions or circumstances, do not let any negative or demeaning communication come from your mouth. Only let those things that are in concert with God's Word come from your mouth. Pray each day that the Lord would give you the strength and the wherewithal to stand firmly on His Word and declare with your mouth and believe in your heart that God is with you and because God is on your side, you are victorious in every way.

Reading Assignment: Read Philippians 2:1-11 before the group session.

*Memory Verse: Phil. 1:21-*For to me to live is Christ, and to die is gain.

Day 1

Act Like You Belong At The Top!

In the fall of 2013, the University of Texas made a decision that sent shock waves running through the flatlands and hills of Texas that felt like an earthquake registering 8.2 on the scale. The only problem is that Texas doesn't sit on enough fault lines to ever face a severe quake. However, what Texans did feel was the closing of a door on the tenure of legendary head football coach Mack Brown and the hiring of his replacement Charlie Strong. At first mention, nothing seems to shake anything up about this choice at all. However, the shock waves came when the news was released that Strong was an African American. The aftershock that is still sending tremors throughout the state and across NCAA College football is this, Coach Strong is the first Black man in the school's illustrious history to hold the head coaching job at the University.

When Coach Strong met his team for the first time, he made it clear that there would be no missing classes, no missing practices, there would be no facial hair or hair weaved flowing from the back of any player's helmet. Coach Strong also made it clear that if they were going to play on his team that a suit and tie would be worn to every game and following every game. He told his squad that if they wanted to be at the top, they had to get used to acting like they belong there!

Read Philippians 1:27-28

The word "conversation" used in verse 27 comes from the Greek word "politeo." We borrow our English term "politics" from it. The root meaning of this word deals emphatically with how you behave like a Christian. In what ways has the behavior of other Christians caused you to stumble in the faith?

Who have you observed blessed you because of his or her faith in Jesus Christ?

Unity is a huge team term. You will never win it without it. How important is striving together in the faith with other believers to you?

Who are some people you are teamed up with right now who make a positive difference in your life?

Who are some people you need to cut from your roster because they are really not good for you at all? Be honest.

Read 2 Corinthians 5:17

When Paul mentions being a "new creature in Christ," what does this mean to you?

Daily Prayer:

Lord, my life may be the only Bible my family and friends will ever read. I pray today that when they see me that they see you in me. Continue to mold me into your image and make me more like Jesus Christ each day. Take out of me those things that you have no need of and place in my life those things that you see fit to deposit. Use my life for your glory, in the name of Jesus Christ, Amen.

Your Journal
Prayers, Thoughts & Notes:

Day 2

Are You Hurt Or Are You Injured?

At first glance, the two terms seem one in the same. Hurt and injured seem to connote and suggest the literary parallel of that of a jacket and a blazer. However, there's much more in these two words than what meets the eye. In every game, there are people who get hurt, and there are people who are injured. The difference between the two is that if you are hurt, you can get up and keep on playing while you are in pain. But, if you are injured, you must retreat to the sideline and get off of the field of play.

As believers in Jesus Christ, we are called to "suffer for his sake" (Phil. 1:29b). In short, there are times when we get hurt. You can get hit by sickness, dropped by job loss, and even blind-sided by things that you just never saw coming. Whatever the case, in the game of life you will get hurt from time to time; however, a game changer is one that knows how to suffer and still come out on top.

Read Philippians 1:29-30

Have you ever suffered while really trying to be faithful to the Lord? Take a devotional moment and look at what caused you the pain.

When you suffered as a Christian did you have moments where you doubted God or even questioned Him? Be honest.

One of the pillar tenants of the Christian faith is belief. Paul mentions it in verse 29. When your faith was tested with suffering, did your belief in the Lord increase or decrease? If you got stronger, why do you think that happened? If you got weaker, why do you think that happened?

Why do you think God allows believers to suffer and live life hurt from time to time?

Christians that have seen some of life's toughest times often have a story to tell. Take a moment and reflect on your story. As you look back over life's journey thus far, spend some time with God right now honoring Him for keeping you alive and allowing you to remain in the game!

Read: Psalms 34:19

Afflictions are a guarantee in the Christian faith. However, the promise of God being our deliverer gives hope. Spend a moment meditating on God as a great deliverer.

Daily Prayer:

Lord, there have been days in my life when things were really tough, but you were there for me. Thank you for moments that I have been hurt in life. The pain caused me to trust you and love you even more. God, if I must face ridicule, misunderstanding and total sacrifice for your sake, I will. You gave your life for me and this day I earnestly vow my life to you in return. Bless me O God, and use me is my prayer. In the name of Jesus, Amen.

Your Journal
Prayers, Thoughts & Notes:

Day 3

Don't Lose In The Locker Room!

The 2014 NBA Championship appeared to belong to the Miami Heat. After all, the game pitted the same two teams in the Championship as it did the year before, the Heat against the Spurs. But something went wrong. The San Antonio Spurs didn't just win the Championship; they dominated the Heat and sent them back to Florida to get a tan. Lebron James, as a free agent, returned to Cleveland and the once famed dream team of Miami, had been dismantled. What happened to the Heat? Some say that the bench for the Spurs was just too hot for the Heat to handle and others contend that Chris Bosh, Dwayne Wade and Lebron James just didn't show up. But, a closer look at the outcome reveals the truth. There was contention and strife in the locker room that caused the Heat to lose the Championship once they hit the floor. In short, the Heat didn't just lose on the floor while the cameras were rolling; they lost in the locker room before they ever came out to play the game.

Here's a great devotional question to ponder, what's going on in your locker room? When you pause to consider the people who make up your inner circle at home, on your job, in the community and at church, how are things going in your locker room?

Read Philippians 2:1-2

The first locker room for most Christians is found in the home. What are some things that cause tension under your roof?

Paul admonishes the church at Philippi to love and unity. What can you do to work faithfully towards that end in your home?

Church congregations are often our extended families and rightfully so. What locker room tension exists in your church family that is an issue for you right now?

How could God use you to help resolve this tension and cause healing and wholeness that would bless everyone in the locker room?

Read St. John 13:34-35

Love is the key to healing relationships that are strained. Plan out a private locker room strategy to love people in your inner circle who are very difficult to get along with, and then put that plan to practice.

Daily Prayer:

Lord, help me to love in such a way that it causes healing, unity, harmony, and synergy to exist everywhere that I am. Empower me with your presence in such a way that when people in my inner circle come near me that they actually encounter you. I love you, I know that you love me, now please help me love others. In the name of Jesus, Amen!

Your Journal
Prayers, Thoughts & Notes:

Day 4

It's Not About You!

Pride is one of the most dangerous attitudes any person can ever have. When pride sets in, it causes an individual to assess falsely what he or she can produce to the point that he or she feels like it's all about him or her. Such was the case with one of the world's greatest sprinters, Marion Jones. She was an Olympic champion and a role model for athletes around the world, but admitted to using illegal sports-enhancing drugs that cost her and her teammates everything. Jones admitted openly that she did not always use sports-enhancing drugs. She says that she became so pressed to win that she forgot about her team, her family and her moral virtue. The good news at present is that Jones is now using her past failures to help others succeed in their futures. The message that she is sharing with the youth that she lectures is simple. It's not about you!

Look at your life for a moment. Can you celebrate when God blesses your neighbor? Are you happy when your friend is promoted? When people near you find favor with God and man, how do you really feel deep down within?

Read Philippians 2:3

Paul says that nothing should be done in "vainglory" or better put, it shouldn't be done for the purpose of people applauding you. Why do you think this kind of glory is considered vain?

Let's be honest for a moment. It is human nature for people to like the spotlight. How can the spotlight be a dangerous place for you?

Humility is not just the opposite of pride it is also the absence of it. In what ways can you express humility in everything that you do? List at least five.

One way to avoid pride and remain humble is to encourage constantly others to be stronger and to achieve more. Make a list of three people you would like to encourage and contact them before the close of the day just to tell them how much they mean to you. This may be done via cell phone, Facebook, Instagram, twitter, phone call or in person.

Read: Proverbs 29:23

Human pride is a sin and lends itself to destruction, but humility causes a believer to flourish. In what ways can you see the benefit of humility in your life?

Daily Prayer:

Lord, I realize that without you being with me that I am nothing. I know that every blessing that I now possess came from you. Forgive me for moments of vanity and personal pride. God, cause humility to rest within me so that my glory is not vain but well placed. You O Lord, deserve all of the glory and the honor. Now God, use me to esteem others greater than I esteem myself. Bless me only so that I might be a blessing. In the name of Christ Jesus, Amen!

Your Journal
Prayers, Thoughts & Notes:

Day 5

I Can't Resist An Assist!

It happens on the court when a player could shoot the ball and score the points as a solo act. But, instead of taking the shot, he passes the ball to a teammate and he scores the points for the team. This is called an assist. It is an unselfish act of kindness shown from one player to another for the sake of blessing the entire team. When the word "assist" is mentioned in the NBA, one name stands out as simply elite. He is in a class all by himself. John Stockton finished his illustrious 19-year career with nearly 16,000 assists! Can you imagine that? Stockton passed the ball to a teammate 15,806 times for him to score instead of taking a shot. Why did he do it you ask? He couldn't resist the assist. John Stockton spent his life on the court making other players play better. He wasn't trying to become the league's leading scorer. He simply made his teammates greater because he fed them with assists that made them score!

Some people in the Christian faith are stingy. There's just no other way to put it. But, this is not the way of the Lord. When we mature as believers, we care more about what God does for others than we do about what He does for ourselves.

Read: Philippians 2:4

No one gets where they are without the assistance of someone else. Take a moment as you have devotion and consider people who assisted you. Who were they?

When you consider all of the things that the Lord has done for you, do you have a lot to be thankful for?

People have assisted you to get where you are. Now here's a soul searching devotional question to consider. Who have you bothered to assist? If you have assisted others be honest and ponder this question, could you be doing more? If so, why aren't you doing it?

Look at the people who are in your immediate family, what could you do right now to make their lives better?

Read: 1 Peter 3:18

The greatest assist time will ever record was the one Jesus tendered at the cross. Jesus died voluntarily so that you could live in Him victoriously. Now that's an assist! He caught death so that you could have life. He caught sin so that you could have salvation! He caught the worst so that you could have the best! Right now think of some people who need God and intercede for them in prayer asking the Lord of heaven to use you to assist them.

Daily Prayer:

Lord of heaven and earth, I bow this day to say thank you for saving me. When I was lost you redeemed me and when I was wounded you restored me. I cannot say thank you enough. God, my prayer this day is for those that I could assist but for whatever reason I have not. Lord, give me just one more chance to bless them, and I will succeed in sharing your love with them in ways that I pray would change their lives just as you have changed mine. I love you Lord. I really do! In Jesus' name, Amen!

Your Journal
Prayers, Thoughts & Notes:

WEEK 3

KEEP PLAYING THE FIGHT SONG!

Let this mind be in you, which was also in Christ Jesus: who, being in the form of God, thought it not robbery to be equal with God: but made himself of no reputation, and took upon him the form of a servant, and was made in the likeness of men: and being found in fashion as a man, he humbled himself, and became obedient unto death, even the death of the cross. Wherefore God also hath highly exalted him, and given him a name which is above every name: That at the name of Jesus every knee should bow, of things in heaven, and things in earth, and things under the earth; and that every tongue should confess that Jesus Christ is Lord, to the glory of God the Father (Phil 2:5-11).

There is nothing like an NCAA football game between two teams that are rivals. Statistics don't matter, records are thrown out of the window, and all that counts is what's on the scoreboard at the end of the game. It is a matter of bragging rights and pride. When Army plays Navy, when Auburn meets Alabama, when Michigan faces off against Ohio State, when Texas kicks off against Texas A&M, when USC finally gets to Notre Dame and when Harvard plays Yale the game is on! Matchups like these are considered classics. Such is the case when two schools from Louisiana meet up in the Crescent City of New Orleans for the Bayou Classic. It is where the Jaguars of Southern hit the field against the Tigers of Grambling.

It is November 27, 1999, and the Superdome is packed to capacity. The Grambling State Tigers are completely dominating the game under head coach Doug Williams all of the way until the latter part of the 3rd quarter. The momentum shifted like a sudden storm that would fall on the Sea of Galilee. Some will say that it was the Jaguar fans shouting "defense Jags defense" that caused the shift in the game. But, there was another element present. The Southern University marching band known as the Human

Juke Box kept on playing their school's fight song. On every first down they played it, on every defensive stop that brass band shouted it, when their team kicked a field goal they played it again and when the Jaguars scored a touchdown they played it and then would press the crowd to join them singing it. Something in their fight song propelled them to victory. The game ended in the greatest upset in Bayou Classic history! Grambling fell to Southern with a final score of 37 to 31 after trailing for nearly three full quarters of football. Yes, the players fought their hearts out to come from behind and win the game, but it was the fight song that made the difference!

When a team hears its fight song something deep within them starts to click. It is not just the music of the song, but the lyrics that hold the melody together that pushes them to victory. Believe it or not, when Paul writes to the church in Philippi like a great head coach in the huddle of a team that is behind on the scoreboard, he reminds them of their fight song. The words that are recorded in Philippians 2:5-11 are the words of a song that Paul uses to refuel, refocus and revive the church. They were the words of a hymn that he knew would strengthen their hearts as they considered the finished work of Jesus Christ at the cross!

Let's explore this great fight song together!

Week Three

THE GROUP ENCOUNTER

Let's Get Started

1. By now you should know the people in your group. If you have any new members, make them feel welcomed! Now take a moment to share with your group how your week has been. Discuss the impact that your daily devotional time with God is having on your life.
2. It is said that music charms the soul. What song greatly inspires you in the faith?
3. Describe a moment in your life when the lyrics of a song ministered to your heart and gave you strength to endure. What song was it? Why was it important to you?

A Look At The Playbook

Watch DVD for "Group Encounter 3" and complete the section below.

The champion of this great hymn is Jesus Christ and Paul presents Him as a divine _____.

"Let this mind be in you which was also in Christ Jesus" would better read like this: get rid of your present _____ and live with an attitude and disposition of Jesus Christ in your _____.

The mind of Christ is a mind of love, compassion, forgiveness, obedience and _____.

Paul also presents Jesus as the _____ illustration.

The Greek word for "form" used in verse 6 is "morphay." And it does not refer to the shape of a thing, but the essence of the thing regardless of the

_____.

When Paul says that Jesus was in the form of God what he was saying was Jesus was God regardless of His shape. Jesus was _____ in a _____ body.

Always remember this, the essence of a _____ always defines the thing, but the only way to redeem a thing is to become the thing that you need to redeem. In short, _____ became us to save us!

Paul concludes by presenting Jesus as one who deserves total

_____.

"For God hath highly exalted Him and hath given Him a name that is above every _____. That at the name of Jesus every knee should bow and every tongue confess that Jesus Christ is _____, to the glory of God the Father."

One great American historian says the greatest names on earth have been those of the men who have led our nation. Call their names, and greatness will surely follow. You do it for yourself. Call the names of George Washington, John Adams, Thomas Jefferson, James Madison, James Munroe, John Q. Adams, and Andrew Jackson. Call the names of Abraham Lincoln, Theodore Roosevelt, Woodrow Wilson, and Calvin Coolidge. Call the names of Herbert Hoover, Franklin D. Roosevelt, Harry S. Truman, Dwight Eisenhower, John F. Kennedy, Lyndon B. Johnson, Richard Nixon, Gerald Ford, Jimmy Carter, Ronald Reagan, George Bush, Bill Clinton, George Bush and Barack Obama.

At His name rejoice as the church celebrates His majesty and His

_____.

The Locker Room Chat

Take a moment to dialogue and discuss as a group the video presentation using the questions below to lead the conversation.

1. The reality of Jesus being God in the flesh is difficult for some people to grasp. This teaching has its roots in the scriptures and is called the Kenosis Doctrine. Kenosis means to empty oneself. God the Father emptied Himself into God the Son. This was done so that the Son of God would become the son of man, so that sons of men might become the sons of God. Discuss this wonderful teaching with your group.
2. Jesus humbled Himself to the degree that He would die like a criminal on a cross for you. Discuss the Kingdom concept of humility. How humble are you willing to become for God to use you?
3. It seems that the humility of Jesus Christ prepared His life for service to His Father. In what ways do you serve God?
4. The essence of God is one God, but the personality of God is triune. He is a loving Father, a beloved Son and a powerful Spirit. Paul teaches us in verse 9 that God highly exalted Jesus and gave Him a name that is above every name. Discuss the role of both God the Father and God the Son in this passage. What did the Father do for His Son?
5. If God the Father highly exalted His own Son Jesus and gave Him a name that is greater than any name, what could you do for the Lord that would highly exalt Him?
6. This entire passage was a great hymn. In what ways do the words of this passage inspire you?

It's Game Time

Prayer Assignment: For the next seven days, seek out ways and means in your life to highly exalt the Lord Jesus Christ. Pray each day until your group meets again for God to grant you opportunities to lift Him up and bless Him. One word of caution, the only way to lift God up is to demote yourself for the purpose of promoting Him. This will require humility. Prayerfully seek out moments for you to seek humility for the purpose of lifting the Lord in your life so that others might see Him and not you.

Reading Assignment: Read Philippians 2:12-30 before the next group session.

Memory Verse: Phil. 2:10 & 11-That at the name of Jesus every knee should bow, of things in heaven, and things in earth, and things under the earth, and that every tongue should confess that Jesus Christ is Lord, to the glory of God the Father.

Week Three

Day 1

Work It Out!

It was a fierce hit and from the looks of it, the career of another great quarterback had come to an end. It was October 20, 2008 when Kansas City Chiefs cornerback Benard Pollard, pounded the knee of the league's leading quarterback, Tom Brady. The hit tore the interior ligaments of his knee apart. It was horrible. Watching the hit made viewers cringe and cover their eyes just looking at it. But, just when everyone thought he would be retiring, Brady underwent surgery and numerous hours of rehabilitation. It was painful and from some perspectives impossible, but with persistence, hard work and consistent labor, the injury made Brady stronger. When asked if he would return to the game that he loved to play, Brady responded by simply saying, "It's an injury, and I plan to work it out!"

Like Brady's knee injury, sin hits every believer hard, and the only way to salvation is for you to work it out through Jesus Christ, Son of the living God!

Read Philippians 2:12-13

Salvation is a free gift that only comes through the person of Jesus Christ. However, Paul says that we must work out our own salvation. What do you think he means by this statement?

It is important for you to remember that there is a huge difference between working out one's salvation and working for one's salvation. As believers in the Lord Jesus Christ, we do not work for our salvation, but we do work out our salvation. By doing this we simply submit our lives to the teachings of Jesus Christ and become conscious, cognizant and committed followers of Him as Master, Lord, Savior and God. With this in mind, look back over your life for a moment at sins that you used to commit. Can you see where you've made some decisions not to do certain things anymore? If so, what are they?

What are some things that you need to lay aside right now that would help you get closer to the Lord? Be honest with your answer.

In verse 13 Paul affirms the fact that the Lord is the one doing all of the work in you each moment of your life. God is in you working it out for you! In what ways have you sensed God's presence in your life changing you, rearranging you and causing you to become more and more like Jesus Christ?

Read Philippians 1:6

When Paul says that "….He that hath begun a good work in you will perform it….," what does that say to you?

As a believer in the resurrected and crucified Christ, you are saved! But, God is still working on you to produce a model of Him in you. It is what is called sanctification. In what ways do you sense right now that the Lord is working on your life?

Daily Prayer:

Lord, I know you are at work in my life. I know it because I am reading the Bible, reading this book and growing closer to you each day. Jesus, as I get closer to you help me to become more and more like you. Help me O Lord, to work out my salvation so that when I am finished with my journey in time I can hear your welcoming voice say to me, "Servant, well done." In the name of Jesus Christ, I humbly pray these petitions. Amen.

Your Journal
Prayers, Thoughts & Notes:

Day 2

I'm Not Doing All Of This For Nothing!

Gabrielle Christina Victoria Douglass took the world by storm in the summer Olympic Games of 2012. Winning two gold medals, she proved to the world with her 4 foot 8-inch frame that hard work pays off. While many of her peers were watching television, playing video games, texting, chatting, dating or just having a good time, she was at work in the gym. But Gabby, as she is affectionately called, had ulterior motives. She was striving for excellence in private so that when she appeared in public, she would be at her very best. The personal sacrifices of Gabrielle were spent for the purpose of winning it all. In short, she didn't do all that she did in practice for nothing, it was for the gold!

Look at your life. What are you living to accomplish? The goal of the believer should be set to do one thing and one thing only, meet God knowing that you have not run your race in this life in vain.

When people look at you praying, forgiving those that have hurt you, helping those that will never repay you, reading God's Word, persevering through obstacles that should have erased you and giving to help those who may never ever see you but benefit from your grace and gratuity, tell them this, "I'm not doing all of this for nothing!"

Read Philippians 2:14-16

Paul admonishes the church in Philippi to do all things without "...murmurings and disputings" or better put without complaining and fussing.

Take a devotional moment and consider some people you interact with who just rub you the wrong way from time to time. Can you see their faces yet? What can you do differently in Christ that should help you to avoid a confrontation with them?

When you consider the contents of verse 15, it is very clear that the life of every believer should be a light in the world that we live. Paul says that we "….shine as lights in the world." If your life was a light on a scale of 1 (being very dim) to 10 (being extremely bright), rate what your light would look like and be honest. What could you do to let your light shine even brighter?

One of the reasons why the world is so dark today is because it does not have the light of God's Word lighting the way. How important is God's Word in your life? How do you really see the Bible and its contents?

Imagine for a moment that a billionaire would pay you $100.00 for every Bible verse you could quote from memory. How much money would you have?

Paul mentions that believers should "Hold forth the Word of life....." In this passage, it means to lift up the life-giving source of the Word of God. However, consider this; you cannot lift it if you do not know it. Take a moment and write out a plan of what you will do to make learning more of God's Word a priority in your life.

Read Psalms 119:105

Keep this in mind; the Lord's Word is described as both a lamp and a light in the scriptures. A lamp was used for seeing things that were close up, and a light or torch was used to give illumination to those things that were ahead. In what ways has God's Word been both to you in your life?

Daily Prayer:

Eternal God, I bow before you to ask that you bless the labor of my life so that my labor for you is never in vain. Empower me through your Word and help me grow more in the days to come than I have ever grown before. Use me, Father, for your glory. Hide your Word in my heart so that I won't sin against you and bless me in miraculous ways so that the light of your Word shines boldly through the life that I live each day, in the name of Jesus Christ, Amen!

Your Journal
Prayers, Thoughts & Notes:

Day 3

This Makes It All Worthwhile!

No one becomes a champion alone. There are always those persons who work diligently behind the scenes who never have their names called, but they sacrifice themselves for the good and blessing of others. It is the summer of 2014, and the B.T. Striders Track Club from Beaumont, Texas left the Lone Star State to participate in the Junior Olympic Games in Iowa. The team is led by a husband and wife, coaches Jeff and Pat Hulon, who sacrifice themselves tirelessly to make a positive difference in the lives of area youth. Once the team arrived at the Junior Olympics, two of the children from the B.T. Striders Track Club earned medals and a national rank! When Jeff and Pat looked at the kids from Beaumont on the medal platform receiving ribbons and awards, they grabbed a camera, took some pictures and sent them to some of their friends and supporters back home.

You see, Jeff and Pat didn't receive any medals. They never called Coach Pat's name, but they both had a sense of joy rushing through their hearts as they watched kids that they had sacrificed to train win and do well in a national competition. When they looked at those kids standing on the platform in Iowa at that moment they had to say to themselves, "This makes it all worthwhile!"

Read Philippians 2:17-18

Joy is not just an emotional feeling, it is a fact of our faith. However, it is sometimes felt when you can see the good that you have caused in the lives of other people. As you spend some quiet time with God, ponder this query, what in your life has been your greatest joy?

Joy in our culture is a terribly misplaced term. People call alcoholic beverages "joy juice" and some think that joy is only a dishwashing detergent. What is joy to you?

What brings Paul joy according to verse 17 is knowing that his life has meaning as it relates to serving the Lord as he serves others. Take a moment and consider some ways that you could help someone who could not help you in return. Who could you help? What would you do for them? How would this act of Christian service bring you joy?

Read James 1:2

The more you count, the more joy you will have. List at least five good reasons that you have joy in your life today:

1. _____
2. _____
3. _____
4. _____
5. _____

Lord Jesus, thank you for this moment of personal devotion with you. I love you, and I am seriously aware of your blessings and favor on my life. God, I do not want to be a reservoir of your goodness, keeping it all to myself. I want to be a channel of blessings! I desire for your favor to both come to me and for your favor to flow through me. Lord, cause me to be a blessing today in the life of someone who needs to know that you still care. In the name of Him who reigns, I pray. In Jesus' name, Amen!

Your Journal
Prayers, Thoughts & Notes:

Day 4

Don't Panic, Help Is On The Way!

It's 1966, and Texas Western University is an unheard of academic institution located in the dusty town of El Paso, Texas. No one knew the school existed until head basketball coach, Don Haskins, showed up on the scene. Haskins strolled onto the campus with limited coaching experience, having only coached girls' basketball, and little to no money to recruit with. He needed help! Just when all seemed hopeless, Haskins did the unthinkable. He started recruiting young African-American athletes with great talent and superior basketball skills to play on his team. Of course, this decision was met with a great deal of controversy by his peers, the general public and the media. But his decision paid off big time. Coach Haskins' help on the court led by five young Black men helped Texas Western University win the NCAA Basketball Championship over famed player Pat Riley and the University of Kentucky by a score of 72-65.

Help from God often comes in strange packages. If Coach Haskins would have denied the help that God supplied for him, he would never have ever won a championship. Thank God for the help that He sends us along the way.

Read Philippians 2:19-24

The help that God sends to the church at Philippi through the Apostle Paul is a young man. According to the passage you just read, what was his name?

Timothy is a young man, and he doesn't have much experience. But, he's the helper God is sending to make a difference. Have you ever needed help and God sent you someone that seemed really unqualified? Why do you think that God does this from time to time?

There are two books in the Bible that bear the name of the help that God gave to the church of Philippi. Look through the Bible and write down the name of both books.

Where in your life do you need the most help? Now ponder this query for just a moment. Could it be that the Lord has already sent help your way to bless you, but you missed it because the help God sent you just didn't look right?

Read 1 Samuel 17:48-51

Israel needed help with Goliath and God sent them David. How did David help them? Why did Israel almost miss the help that God sent them?

Daily Prayer:

Lord of heaven, I need help in many areas of my life. Send help my way God, and cause me to recognize that they are sent from you; make me receptive to what they have to say and responsive in what I need to do. Thank you, O God, for being my help in ages past and my help in years to come. You are my help, my shield and my victory. In the name of Jesus Christ, Amen!

Your Journal
Prayers, Thoughts & Notes:

Day 5

Miracles Still Happen!

Kevin Everett is a native of Port Arthur, Texas and a graduate of Thomas Jefferson High School. He was always a super athlete, and the people from the "Trill," as Port Arthur is always called, knew that Everett would make it big, and he did. In 2005, he was drafted by the Buffalo Bills as a tight end! Fast-forward to NFL opening day, September 7, 2007, the Bills are pitted against the Broncos from Denver. It's the first game of the season, the first play of the season; it's the kickoff and Everett is on the field tackling the return man for the Broncos, Domenik Hixon. From the moment of impact, Everett's body fell lifelessly to the ground. A hush fell over the stadium. Coaches, trainers and medical staff rushed to his aid.

As his motionless body lay on the field, it became clear that his injuries were life threatening. The initial report was that Everett had sustained a serious fracture and dislocation of his spine and would probably never walk again. Fans, friends and those in the faith started to pray fervently for Kevin. Orthopedic surgeon Dr. Andrew Cappucino made it clear that Everett had undergone injuries that could have taken his life, but was recuperating miraculously. On December 23, 2007, just a few months after many thought Kevin would never walk again, he walked into Ralph Wilson Stadium showing the world that miracles still happen!

There are those who argue and contend that miracles no longer happen. However, the scriptures are clear. Miracles happen every day!

Read Philippians 2:25-30

In verse 25, Paul presents a man whose name is Epaphroditus. What words are used to describe him by the great Apostle?

Why do you think Epaphroditus should be seen as a miracle (Hint: Read vs. 26-27)?

A miracle is best defined as a transcendent occurrence that it takes the hand of God to produce. With this in mind, have you ever seen God's hand produce a miracle? Has God ever performed a miracle for you?

There are people you may know of right now who stand in need of a miracle. Who are they? What do they need from the Lord?

Read Ephesians 3:20-21

The power and authority of God is like nothing the earth has ever seen. Look carefully at the words used by Paul in this verse. What do they mean to you?

Daily Prayer:

Lord Jesus, you have been and still remain the greatest physician time has ever seen. God, you are a miracle worker. You are the same yesterday, today, and forever and for me that means you still give sight to the blind, make the lame to walk, make the deaf hear and make diseases disappear. God, I lift those to you today that others said would never get any better. Heal them with your touch and restore them with your hand. And, when you do it, give me the strength to shout glory so that I may honor you. Thank you Lord, for who you are and what you can do, in the name of Jesus Christ, Amen!

Your Journal
Prayers, Thoughts & Notes:

WEEK 4

HE BIT ME!

Finally, my brethren, rejoice in the Lord. To write the same things to you, to me indeed is not grievous, but for you it is safe. Beware of dogs, beware of evil workers, beware of the concision. For we are the circumcision, which worship God in the spirit, and rejoice in Christ Jesus, and have no confidence in the flesh (Phil 3:1-3).

It is the most popular game in the known world in that it transcends every culture and socio-economic barrier. It connects people from different countries; it pulls people together who have different languages, and it forces those who are competitive in spirit to try it at least. Kids from all seven continents play it with a passion as if the patched ball on the field of play is all that matters. Men play this game for the love of the sport and bragging rights. It is the game of all games for most of the people who play it, from the mud huts of the Sudan to the freezing corridors of Switzerland, from the wealthy boundaries of the US to the economically challenged nation of Haiti, people play this game. Unlike tennis, golf or cricket, this game is a game for everyone. This game is known to most as football, but in the United States of America it is called soccer.

In every sport, there is an ultimate championship. In the NFL, it is called the Super Bowl; in baseball, it is called the World Series; in Hockey, it is called the Stanley Cup; in the CFL, it is called the Grey Cup; but in soccer, The Holy Grail for the overall winner is the World Cup. In the summer of 2014, nations paused as some of the greatest athletes in the known world gathered in the country of Brazil for the FIFA World Cup. The pageantry was breathtaking; the competition was fierce and country pride was on the line in every game. In short, in each round of competition, the field of soccer became a battleground filled with bruises, blisters and some broken bones. But, in one competition, things became so intense that there was even biting happening on the field of play. Not just a coach nervously nibbling on a towel as his team missed a close shot that should have been a score, but biting that occurred when one player decided that he would chew on his opponent without any salt or pepper being added to the meal.

It happened on June 24, 2014 when soccer player Luis Suarez, decided that he'd had enough of Georgio Chiellini. As both players made their way to midfield, Suarez found a way to bite Chiellini on the shoulder. At first glance, it appeared to be just another incidental collision on the soccer field, but upon closer investigation, it was very intentional. Chiellini grabbed his shoulder and yelled loudly enough for the crowd to hear his cry, "Ahhhhh, he bit me!"

For a FIFA World Cup game, it was a first. A soccer player that bites! It may have been a first for FIFA, but it was not a first for many of the millions of people watching the game as spectators. Let's be honest; some of the people we have encountered in life have some canine characteristics, and they too bite like evil demon-possessed animals. As we enter chapter 3 of Paul's letter to the church at Philippi, he warns the believers of that city against people who show up in life that are dogs. They are people who growl all of the time, bark too much and threaten to bite whenever possible.

Has it ever happened to you? Have you ever been bitten before by people you thought you could trust? How did you handle it? The teachings of this passage are designed to empower every believer to know how to cope, conquer and overcome difficult people who are close to you every day.

Week Four

THE GROUP ENCOUNTER

Let's Get Started

1. Take a moment and gather with the people who are in your group. Today ask each person for a simple prayer request and begin with a whisper of prayer for those things that are needed for each person in the group.
2. There are times in life when we are hurt by people. Discuss an occasion where this has happened to you.
3. Why do you think that God allowed it happen?
4. Why should you be careful when in the company of vicious people?

A Look At The Playbook

Watch DVD for "Group Encounter 4" and complete the section below.

If you are not careful, they will steal your _____.

Paul says in the passage "_____." The Greek should translate like this, "as for the rest of what I was trying to say."

Here it is again, he says rejoice in the _____. Why on earth would you tell a group full Christians to rejoice? Here is the answer, because the enemy is always trying to _____ it.

Jesus Christ is the _____, _____ and the _____ of true joy!

If you are not careful, they will make you lose your
_____.

Paul says the same word three times in chapter 3:2. He says
_____. The Greek word is "blepo." It means to
_____ without blinking.

If you are not careful, they will rob you of your _____.

A dog responds best when you call its _____.

You can tell people who possess a canine spirit by simply watching what
happens when you _____ their names. They love hearing
their names called.

Paul refers to real believers in 3:3 as the _____. Retranslation
– we are the real deal! How do you know? Because we worship God in
the _____, we _____ in Jesus Christ and have no
confidence in the flesh.

The Locker Room Chat

Take a moment to dialogue and discuss as a group the video presentation
using the questions below to lead the conversation.

1. Have you ever encountered any people who were "dogs"? Where
   were you? What happened? Did they bite you?
2. Be honest, how did you respond to them? Did you strike back?
   What did you do?
3. After reading this passage of scripture and sharing this video
   presentation, what will you do when faced with "dogs" the next
   time?
4. Confidence in the flesh produces pride. In what ways have you
   ever seen pride sneak into your life?
5. In what ways can religious pride be dangerous? Discuss your
   answer.

It's Game Time

Prayer Assignment: For this week's assignment, you will need a clean sheet of paper, a used plastic water bottle and some prayer time. For the next seven days, your prayer assignment will be to pray for people who have caused intentional and unintentional hurt in your life. This will start off painful but by mid-week, you will notice that the pain will produce a pathway to healing and deliverance. Begin the assignment by simply making a list of the people you have found it difficult to forgive. You may even want to write brief descriptions of what they did to cause you hurt and pain. When your list is complete, pray for every person on it, rip it into shreds, place the shreds into a used plastic bottle and throw it in the trash. Just as you are separated from the bottle where the hurt is written so will you be delivered from the hurt they inflicted.

Reading Assignment: Read Philippians 3:4-7

Memory Verse: Phil. 3:2-Beware of dogs, beware of evil workers, beware of the concision.

Week Four

Day 1

Stats Don't Win Games!

Statistics is best defined as numeric and sequential data regarding teams, individual athletes, groups and other entities that utilize mathematical portion to paint pictures of likely possibility. In the world of sports, these pictures of possibility are called stats. Before every game, sports announcers, enthusiasts, and commentators alike take a look at the stats to see who should win the game before the contest ever takes place. It's April 1997, and a relatively new golfer has hit the scene by the name of Eldrick Tont Woods whose alias is Tiger. He steps onto the course to play the Masters and by all of the statistics, there was no way for him to win it. After all, he was too young, lacked experience at that level of play and his competition was anything but mediocre. But somehow against both the stats and the facts, Woods won it all! History reflects the fact that he was the youngest golfer in PGA history at that time to win the Masters.

There are times in life when the stats are stacked against you. What should you do? Here's the answer to that question and don't ever forget it, play the game and play to win!

Read Philippians 3:4-6

The Apostle Paul openly admits that if his stats could have made him a winner that he would have been in first place. Look closely at verse 5 and write down Paul's greatest stats.

1. _____
2. _____
3. _____
4. _____
5. _____

Why do you think that stats cannot and will not ever determine the winner of a contest?

Here's the answer to the above-listed question. Stats are portraits of what has happened in the past and God never lets your past determine what your future looks like. Take a moment to look at some of the mistakes in your past that you have overcome. What are they? What did you learn from them?

Some people have to play the game of life with the odds stacked against them. Take a moment to list at least four of the most difficult odds that were stacked against you that the Lord helped you to overcome.

1. _____

_____

2. _____

_____

3. _____

_____

4. _____

_____

The stats of Paul's life are very impressive. His accomplishments were excellent yet he has reached a point where he understands that only what you do for Jesus Christ will last. Have you reached this point in your life yet? Be honest with your answer.

Read 1 John 4:4

Never forget this Kingdom principle, what's great about you is not what you have accomplished, but what the Lord of heaven has accomplished for you that you could not have never accomplished for yourself. Here's a Kingdom truth that should remain with you forever, Jesus paid it all! He alone deserves the honor and the recognition!

Daily Prayer:

Lord of heaven, there are days that I can sense that the odds are stacked against me, and the stats don't favor me. But as long as you favor me, I will always be victorious. Thank you, Lord Jesus, for the many accomplishments that you have blessed me to achieve, thus far, in my life, but I know that without you I am nothing. As I pray right now, my soul is humbled to know that you have given me so much. I rejoice because I know that I owe everything to you! I love you Lord God! In the name of your Son and my Savior Jesus Christ I pray, Amen!

Your Journal
Prayers, Thoughts & Notes:

Day 2

Sometimes You Lose To Win!

Imagine for a moment there was a job description posted on the Internet. The duties of the job were as follows:

RESPONSIBLE FOR THE FOLLOWING: All Accounts Receivable, Accounts Payable, General Ledger, Payroll Accounting and monitoring all fiscal affairs of the organization. Provide fiscal projections for the entire entity and develop accurate details of the usage of all funds that are to be utilized. Provide Counseling (Psychiatric and Psychological) on an as-needed basis, Mentoring, Coaching, Guiding and Providing for those who are in need; Leads, Directs, Plans, Organizes, Strategizes, Conceptualizes, Prioritizes, and Implements all of the administrative affairs for all persons present. Provide training in various environments to guarantee good outcomes for all persons trained. Oversee, lead and be responsible for those who are under your leadership. Produce and procure a safe, healthy, user-friendly environment that is conducive for growth, strength and personal development. Dictate, educate, and provide discipline for those who are not cooperative without losing anyone in the process. Give governance to the overall health, wealth and well-being of persons present and facilities governed. Must provide any additional services on an as-needed basis whenever needed.

WORK HOURS: 24 Hours a Day, 7 Days a Week, 365 Days a Year, Until Death

RATE OF PAY: $ 0.00/annually

Be honest, would you want a job like this? Here's the truth, only a crazy person would take a job like this right? But when you look at the work of a great mother and an awesome father, they do and have done all of the aforementioned things for us and in some cases they have done even more! You see, a real parent loses for their children to win and when their children win, their losing pays off!

Read Philippians 3:7

Paul understands that all of his accomplishments in this life mean nothing if he is not willing to lose them for the sake of Christ. With this in mind, the name of the game is sacrifice. Take a moment and consider the sacrifice Jesus Christ made for you at Calvary. What does this mean to you?

Now take a moment to consider the personal sacrifices that you have made for Jesus Christ. What have you sacrificed for Him that is really noteworthy?

How do you feel about your list of sacrifices? Do you feel like you owe the Lord something that you cannot repay Him? Be honest with your reply.

Like a great parent, God the Son lost at Calvary for believers to win every day of our lives in Him. As a parent, what sacrifices have you made for your children?

Take a deep breath and consider this last question for today's exercise. Imagine you have made it to heaven. And your reward was in one golden box! You now open your box only to discover that only the things that you had sacrificed for Christ on earth were in your box. What would you have when you got to heaven?

Read St. Luke 6:38

In the Kingdom of God, we give to gain. In short, we believe that givers are gainers pure and simple. However, we don't always like giving because it feels like we are losing. But, here's a great Kingdom truth for today, we lose to win! What are some things that you could give the Lord today that would put a smile on His face?

Daily Prayer:

Eternal and all-wise God, I thank you this day for the sacrifice that you made for me that has guaranteed my salvation in Jesus Christ. And I thank you for the sacrifices that others have made for me so that I could have what I have right now. O God, help me to give more of me to you for the sacrifice and blessing of others. Lord, I am willing to lose so that my sacrifice will empower others to win! In the name of Jesus, Amen!

Your Journal
Prayers, Thoughts & Notes:

Day 3

What You Know Makes The Difference!

Knowledge is always the difference maker. It is 2005, and Serena Williams is trying to make a comeback. Her 2004 year was a disaster to say the least. She is determined to make her game the best that it can be. She has struggled in the past with making the right plays at the right time to earn victories in tough match sets. But 2005 would be different. Serena begins her year with the Australian Open against the famed and hardworking Maria Sharapova. The sets are heated, and the match is tough but Serena pulls it out and wins the entire Open. While being interviewed, she was asked what made the difference in her performance. Her response shocked everyone in the audience. Williams simply said, "What you know is what makes the difference!"

We cannot be for certain what Serena Williams meant by her comment, but what we do know is that theologically she is completely accurate. Knowledge of who God is, what God is, how God works, what God has said and what the Lord has done for you is key to victory in a believer's life.

Read Philippians 3:8-11

When you really love someone you want to know them even more. Take a moment and list at least seven things that you KNOW about God:

1. _____
2. _____
3. _____
4. _____
5. _____

6. _____
7. _____

Paul states in verse 8 that he "counts all things but loss for the excellency of the knowledge of Christ…..that I may win Christ." What does this statement mean in your heart?

Here's something all believers should know, self-righteousness is always bad. This is because no human being on the earth is completely flawless. All of us have made some mistakes. However, when we become believers in Jesus Christ by faith, the righteousness of God stands for us so that we are righteous in the sight of God. This is called the imputed righteousness of God. Read Romans 4:23-25.

Re-read verse 10. Paul's desire in life is just to know Jesus Christ. However, if he is an Apostle, one would think that he already knew Jesus Christ. What do you think Paul means by what he says in the verse?

Here's the answer to the above-listed question. No one knows all that there is to know about Jesus Christ. He is a revealed mystery. The more you know about Him, the more there is to be known. With this in mind, if you could know three hidden things about the Lord, what would they be?

1. _____
2. _____
3. _____

Read Isaiah 55:8-9

Remember these two words: TRANSCENDENT and IMMINENT. The Lord we serve is both at the same time. He is transcendent meaning He is so far above us that He cannot be understood. And He is imminent in that He is close; He walks with you each day.

Daily Prayer:

Lord, you are the love of my life and I want to know you. The more I know about you, the closer I feel to you, and the closer I get to you the more I become like you. God, what I know about you makes a difference in my life every day. I want to know you to the point that you can live your life through me so that when people encounter me in this life, they actually meet you. In the name of Jesus, I submit my petition, Amen.

Your Journal
Prayers, Thoughts & Notes:

Day 4

I Didn't Know It All!

The greatest players of any game never feel like they are good enough. They spend countless hours practicing, watching film and re-reading playbooks. All of the greats know the secret to being even greater: they know that they have not yet arrived at perfection. Peyton Manning, Larry Bird, and Derek Jeter all play different sports. Manning plays football, Bird played basketball and Jeter was great at baseball, but when you look at their success in the sports that they love, they changed the games they were in because they never stopped studying the game. In short, they knew that they didn't know it all.

Not long ago, ESPN did a wonderful story on NFL Hall of Famer Jerry Rice. He was one of the greatest receivers to ever play the game. Rice didn't play his college ball at a Big Ten school. He played for a small school in the Mississippi Delta, Mississippi Valley State University in the one-horse town of Itta Bena. As Rice told his story, he attributed his success to God, his family, hard work and hours of study and film watching. He said, "I love the game. I played it all of my life. But I always knew that I didn't know it all!"

When you think you know it all you know nothing and when you know that you don't know, you make room in your soul to grow and know.

Read Philippians 3:12

The word "attained" Paul used in verse 12a was used in Greek scholarship. It was used by students as a reference to lessons that had

---

been learned. It could be translated like this, "I have taken the classes but I have not graduated." Why do you think Paul feels this way? *(continued)*

In verse 12b, Paul admits that he is not perfect. This is important because perfect people see no need for personal improvement. What are three areas of your life that you want to see improvement? Write them below and be very honest.

1. _____
2. _____
3. _____

When you come to know Jesus Christ, it is safe to say that He has changed your life forever. In short, He has a hold on you and you will spend the rest of your life trying to lay hold on Him. In what ways can you say that Jesus has a grip on your life? Be specific.

Read 2 Timothy 2:15

All real disciples are followers of Jesus Christ and students of the scriptures. If you are going to grow in what you know, you must spend time studying the Word of God. Today make yourself a simple Kingdom promise that you will study your Bible for at least five minutes a day every day for the rest of your life.

My Personal Pledge

I, _____, vow and pledge to make time to read God's Word each day for the rest of my life. I realize that I cannot make it without the Lord and the more I read, study and pray, the stronger I become as a Christian.

I make this vow on the _____ day of _____ in the year of _____.

_____
Name

Daily Prayer:

Lord, I know that I don't know it all, but I want to know as much as I possibly can. God, help me read, study and pray daily. Increase my knowledge of your Word and bless me with wisdom that comes from you. In Jesus' name, Amen.

Your Journal
Prayers, Thoughts & Notes:

Day 5

Leave Them In The Dust!

The 2014 Kentucky Derby read like a fairytale by the time everything was over. After all, the Derby is for wealthy animal owners, with the best pedigree horses, from the best areas of the country. That's how it has been for years. But 2014 would be different. In fact, not many would have ever picked the 2014 Derby winner. Normally, the big guys win the Kentucky Derby but God placed His hand on a horse that was the result of a strange birth. Owners Steve Coburn and Jerry Martin bred an $8,000.00 mare with a $2,500.00 stallion to produce the horse that would win it all. Sounds impossible but it happened. An unheard of horse by the name of California Chrome left the rest of the field behind when he crossed the finish line in first place to take home the money. Chrome didn't come from wealthy owners or pedigree stock. He was just a plain ole racehorse with a will to win.

The owners had a simple philosophy regarding all of their competitors, critics and naysayers and it worked. Their rule of thumb as they trained California Chrome was to "leave them in the dust!"

Read Philippians 3:13

Paul has made up his mind that he is moving forward and the only way to do that is to focus. So he says, "….this one thing I do…." This means that he has one thing on his mind. Here's a great devotional question for you to ponder, what's on your mind?

What role does God play in what's on your mind today?

Paul says that he is "forgetting those things which are behind…" The word "forgetting" comes from the Greek word "epilanthanomai." It is a tongue twister, but it is awesome in meaning. It is a term used in Greco-Roman chariot races where one chariot leaves his opponents in the dust. What are some things that you need to leave in the dust in order for you to continue moving forward with your life? Be specific.

In most cases, races are never won easily. They require that you reach forth with all of your might. In some instances, the winners and losers are decided at the tape as they reach for the finish line. With this in mind, there are some things that you should reach for as a Christian. Listed below is a list of things we should all reach for as believers in Christ. Take a look at the list below and place them in order of importance to you. 1-being most important and 5-being least important:

Financial Well-being   _____
Physical Well-being   _____
Family Relationships   _____
Service to God   _____
Personal Goals   _____

Look back at your list; do you need to make any real adjustments? If so, what are they?

Read St. Matthew 6:33

<u>**Daily Prayer:**</u>

Lord of heaven and God of glory, I bless your name and I reach for you with all of my heart, soul and mind. I thank you for being patient with me as I work to make the life that you are giving to me pleasing unto you. I am not perfect, but Lord, it is my desire to please you in every way. Father, give me the strength to leave my pain, problems and pitfalls in the dust of my life and help me to run onward and upward doing all that I can do, while I can do it. Grant me your favor and bless me with more focus and faithfulness towards you. In the name of my Savior, Jesus Christ, I pray it all. Amen!

Your Journal
<u>**Prayers, Thoughts & Notes:**</u>

WEEK 5

'VE GOT MY SECOND WIND!

I press toward the mark for the prize of the high calling of God in Christ Jesus (Phil. 3:14).

A marathon is not just an ordinary race. It is a race only for those who can endure. Antiquity has it put that marathons have their historical root in Greco-Roman legend when a messenger by the name of Pheidippides ran all of the way from the battlefield of Marathon to Athens without stopping to declare the Persians had been defeated. History has it that he ran into the Greek counsel shouting "hupernikeo," which is to be translated: we have overcome them with victory. It was a twenty-six mile run then, and it is still a twenty-six mile run today.

Like Phedippides ran in years past, Americans are running like crazy these days. We run for exercise, some run for fun and many run to compete. One of the most celebrated competitions in America today is the Boston Marathon and on April 15, 2013, we were left with a memory we will never forget. It was a beautiful day with scores of qualified runners from all over the world set to run through the city on a 26-mile journey that would leave only person a true winner. The race had just gotten underway when not one, but two pressure cooker bombs exploded filled with lead bearings, nails and pellets. Three were pronounced dead at the scene; 264 were seriously injured and hospitalized and 16 lost limbs. The scenes were horrific. The CNN footage showed people running and screaming, debris flying, runners falling and massive panic.

The FBI launched a nationwide manhunt and found two Chechen brothers as the culprits. However, the damage was already done. The day was ruined; the race was cancelled and our nation was like a wounded runner who had no breath left. One year later with faith in our hearts and resilience in our spirits, the Boston Marathon 2014 commenced. Only this time, there was a very special group of participants present sporting their newly placed prosthetic limbs. One such participant was a young woman whose name was Celeste Corcoran; she had lost both legs in the explosion of 2013. But she showed up one year later to finish what she had started the year before, this time wearing two prosthetic legs. Celeste embodies a spirit of faith that says when life is hard, the road is tough and you don't think that you go any further; that's when you must get up and find a way to run on.

Celeste did not finish the race in 2013, but she returned in 2014 and finished it with a smile on her face, her daughter holding her hand, and two prosthetic limbs for legs to walk on. She was greeted by a host of friends and family with media personnel all over the place when she crossed the finish line. They took pictures and asked questions of this great woman, and she made it clear that she would not complain about her circumstances. She was happy to be alive. Learning to use her new legs had been a challenge, but she is walking again and that was exciting to her. She admits that she got tired along the way, the process had been grueling, but she said what helped her most is that when she couldn't go any further somehow she got a second wind!

A second wind! What a concept! It is best described by runners in a race when they have reached the point of exhaustion, but somehow they dig deep within and find the strength to run until they finish the race. As Paul writes to the church in Philippi, it is clear that he views himself as a runner who made up in his mind that he is going to finish no matter what because he too has a second wind! He has been imprisoned, but he is still running; he has been misunderstood, but he is still running; he has been beaten and nearly killed, shipwrecked and rejected by many, but he is still running. And not only is he running, but he has announced that he is pressing his way towards the prize for the high calling of God in Christ Jesus!

Life is not a wind sprint. It is a long-distance run, and its only winners are those who endure until the end. However, like runners in a race, we can become weary, desire to stop, throw in the towel and just give up. Be honest and open for a moment, has it ever happened to you? Thank God you are still running because it is clear that you too found a second wind.

What needs to happen to push you to the point of gaining a second wind so that you keep on running in life?

Week Five

THE GROUP ENCOUNTER

Let's Get Started

1. Take a moment to speak to everyone present in your group. Discuss some of your greatest challenges in the week past if any. Take a moment and have group prayer and include those issues.
2. Have you ever faced a moment in your life when you had to just press your waythrough?
3. Paul mentions a "high calling of God" in verse 14. What do you think he means by this?
4. To meet God and be saved should mean everything to you as a believer. How important is this to you right now?

A Look At The Playbook

Watch DVD for "Group Encounter 5" and complete the section below.

You must reach a point of personal _____.

Paul states it on this wise, "I _____."

The word "press" used by Paul in verse 14 is the term "deeoko" in the Greek. It is a portrait of a _____ who is holding nothing back. A runner that is in pursuit of a _____.

The reason Christians must press is because we must learn to run through the _____.

All runners get tired and can become fatigued. It is then that some slow down, others stop and many quit. However, never forget this; there is a _____ in your _____.

You must reach the person of your _____ ambition.

The "mark for the prize" as described by Paul was defined by a finish line or a _____ that was used to mark the end of a race.

The chief idea regarding this prize was not to win the race in first place, but to _____ the race to meet the face at the finish line.

The greatest prize for any believer should be to see the face of _____ when this life is over.

You must reach the place of your eternal _____.

Paul's "high calling of God in Christ Jesus" deals specifically with his _____ in Christ.

The phrase "high calling" in the Greek comes from the word "anoklaysis," and it refers to an _____to a runner to ascend the podium at the end of the race.

The invitation that Paul preached and lived was for _____ to find salvation in the person of Jesus Christ.

The greatest call in life a believer will ever have is a call to become a _____ of the King.

The Locker Room Chat

Take a moment to dialogue and discuss as a group the video presentation using the questions below to lead the conversation.

1. A real runner needs a second wind. As you run this Christian race, have you ever encountered your second wind? What happened? Share your testimony with your group.

2. Imagine for a moment that life is like a race with four laps around a track defined by your age. Lap 1: 0yrs to 18yrs old   Lap 2: 19yrs to 38 yrs old   Lap 3: 39yrs to 68 yrs old   Lap 4: 69 yrs to 100 yrs old. What lap would you be in right now?
3. If you are in laps 3 or 4, how would you like to live the rest of your life? What is the chief aim of your life at this point?
4. Imagine for a moment meeting Jesus Christ at the end of your life. Your race is over, and you have finished it in a way that makes Him pleased with you. What would you say to Him?

It's Game Time

Prayer Assignment: This week's prayer assignment is for you to write out what you would like to do with the life you have remaining. Please keep in mind, that only what you do for Jesus Christ will last. Make a spiritual bucket list. After your list is finished, take a moment and whisper this prayer:

Lord of creation and Christ of the cross, I do not know what your plans for the rest of my life look like. But I want you to know that if you decide to let me live, I would do everything in my power to please you by faithfully performing everything on this list. My list is designed to give your name glory, honor, praise and thanksgiving. I trust you O God, and anyway that you decide to bless me is fine with me. In the name of Jesus Christ, I pray. Amen.

Reading Assignment: Read Philippians 3:15-21

Memory Verse: Phil. 3:14-I press toward the mark for the prize of the high calling of God in Christ Jesus.

Week Five

Day 1

Uniformity Is One Thing, But Unity Is Another!

Looking at teams in uniform is always exciting! The colors, the pageantry, the pride, the meaning and the mascots bring teams to life. But here's a radical truth that never changes for any team no matter what sport they play, just because you have on the same uniform does not mean that the team has unity. Uniforms are worn on the outside, unity comes from the inside; uniforms are the same color, unity means of the same kind; uniforms are designed to make a team look the same, but unity means that they share one main thing that is the same thing. All too often when a team reaches the point of play and the competition rises, the team that has unity prevails against the team that only has on nice uniforms.

Like teams, often in church settings we too have uniforms, but they do not produce unity. Just because the choir is dressed in nice robes does not make the members of the choir have harmony in their relationships; just because all of the deacons where the same tie does not mean that they love each other and just because all of the ushers are dressed in the same apparel does not mean that they have the same mind.

Unity comes with a price tag that far outweighs a great uniform any day of the week!

Read Philippians 3:15-16

Paul admonishes and encourages the church members in Philippi to "....mind the same thing" (vs. 16). Why do you think he told them to do this?

The greatest enemy of God's Kingdom on earth is division. Our Lord stated that a house divided against itself would never stand. Have you ever experienced a group of Christians that have been divided? What happened? Could you have helped the situation? If so, how?

The Apostle Paul wants the believers in Philippi to "….walk by the same rule…" In short, he wants the standards to be the same for everybody. Have you ever seen favoritism destroy a group?

A believer should be a part of a local assembly called a church. If you could pray a prayer for unity in your church what would it be? List areas of your church family that need unity:

1. _____
2. _____
3. _____
4. _____

Read 1 Corinthians 1:10-15

In the Kingdom of God, believers make up a faith family. Just as in family relationships you don't always agree, so it is in Kingdom relationships as well. But hold onto this truth, unity does not mean you always agree, it just means that no matter what you will always hold true those things you have in common.

Daily Prayer:

Take a moment and write a prayer of unity for your family and your church.

_____
_____
_____
_____
_____
_____
_____

Your Journal
Prayers, Thoughts & Notes:

Day 2

Follow The Leader!

When names like Bobby Orr, Gordie Howe, Maurio Lemiuex, Maurice Richard and Doug Harvey are mentioned, you can't help but think about the game of hockey. But there is one name that stands out as elite when you consider the greats that have played the game, for the men who know well how to roll on ice, fight when needed and win at all cost. His name is Wayne Gretzky! Born in Brantford, Ontario in 1961, he was known by both his fans and fierce opponents as "the great one!" He won four Stanley Cups, won MVP numerous times, was the Rookie of the Year when he first hit the ice and was the leading scorer of the game of hockey with a record that is still unbroken, scoring 2,857 points in his career.

Gretzky's greatest asset was not only seen in his ability to score points on the ice but how he could positively influence his teammates while they were with him. One sports enthusiast wrote that what made Wayne Gretzky the greatest hockey player to ever play the game was not just his indescribable thirst to be great, but his insatiable will to make his teammates better by the example that he set for them to follow.

Real leaders are pacesetters, trend makers and life changers. They are people of empowerment. One leadership guru put it on this wise; leaders help you to do what you otherwise would not or could not do without them. In short, real leaders make your life stronger. That's why when you have real leaders in your presence, like Gretzky on the ice, they demand your attention, and they will make you better as you follow their lead.

Read Philippians 3:17

Take a moment and look at your life. Aside from Jesus Christ, who has been the greatest leader in your life? What lessons did you learn from him or her?

Leaders are people of influence and all of us influence someone else. Who are some people that you influence? Here's a deep devotional question to consider. What have you influenced them to do?

Paul encourages the church in Philippi to be "....follower together of me...." Paul had a Pastor's heart and was a great leader, missionary and defender of the Christian faith. As a member of the Lord's Church, you have a Pastor. What difference has your Pastor made in your life?

Some people in a group refuse to follow the leader. Paul says that we should "...Mark..." those that do follow the leader. Why do you feel that he makes this statement?

Read 1 Timothy 2:1-3

Daily Prayer:

As you follow the Lord Jesus Christ, you always want to follow sincere obedient believers who are following Him and run from those who are not. List at least three people who are alive whose faith in God causes you to follow them and whisper a prayer for each of them right now.
Make sure that you include your Pastor and church leaders on your list.

Your Journal
Prayers, Thoughts & Notes:

Week Five

Day 3

In The Heat of Battle!

Heated moments in both life and sports define people. Some people crackup and fall apart when the heat is on, and others rise to the occasion. Such is the case, with a little girl who against all of the odds, public criticism and at times personal slander, has risen to the top of her game. Mo'ne Davis is a 13-year-old superior little league pitcher from Philadelphia, who has faced the heat of national competition and defied the odds as a champion. Many of Davis' critics argued that a girl could never reach such heights and that she had no place in a global competition filled with boys her age. However, proof of her excellence has best been seen in the heat of battle! Mo'ne Davis is the first girl in Little League World Series history to pitch a winning game and the first girl to pitch a shutout.

Heated moments will come, criticism will surface and things can get really tough but when you are prepared for battle and ready for the heat, you emerge as Mo'ne Davis, a champion and a game changer!

Read Philippians 3:18-19

Battlefields are always heated. As a believer in Jesus Christ, you are on the battlefield every day of your life. There are many who are critics of the cross and what you believe as a Christian. How have you have handled this kind of heat in your life?

Preparation is the key to victory in any battle. How do you prepare for spiritual battle each day? What are some things that you need to do to become even stronger?

In verse 19, Paul gives some characteristics of people who are enemies of the cross. Take a moment and re-read the verse and list their characteristics in the spaces below:

1. _____
2. _____
3. _____
4. _____

It is getting harder and harder for real Christians to be real Christians. Some subjects that surface around you as a believer in Jesus Christ bring controversy to the forefront and the heat of battle commences. With this in mind, have you ever had a conversation about?

- Abortion
- Homosexuality
- Adultery
- Fornication
- Suicide
- Israel
- Immigration

If so, where did you stand on those issues? Keep this in mind, as believers in Jesus Christ, we are called to stand where Jesus Christ stood on every issue.

Read St. Matthew 5:43-48

Daily Prayer:

Lord, my love for you, causes me to face people who are enemies of the cross and those that despise me because of my faith. Give me the strength to rise in the heat of battle like smoke from a furnace. Make me strong enough to stand for your Word, your Will and your Way no matter what. I pray right now for those who have sought evil towards me and even dislike me for reasons beyond my control. I have chosen to love them and forgive. More than that, O God, it is my assignment from you to stand on the battlefield while you fight my battle for me! Therefore, Lord of Hosts, fight on! Just grant me I pray O Lord, the wherewithal to stand no matter what. In the name of Jesus, Amen!

Your Journal
Prayers, Thoughts & Notes:

Week Five

Day 4

This Was Great But I Miss Home!

South Chicago can be a very difficult part of the windy city to live in. After all, poverty is immense, the crime rate is high and the drug scene is horrible. Yet from what some would consider being inner city ruins has risen a group of young boys who have changed history forever. The Illinois Little League Baseball team from Chicago was crowned winners of the Little League World Series from the United States during the summer of 2014. Make no mistake about it, we have had winners from this country before, but nothing like these kids. They were the first all-African-American Little League Baseball team to accomplish such a feat. Just when people around the country were starting to ask, "Can anything good come out of South Chicago," a reply from the hearts of some kids who worked hard and won it all shouted loudly enough for the entire world to hear them, "Yes!"

The pitcher from the Chicago team told a reporter that this season has been a dream come true for their team. He said, "This stuff was great, but I miss home!" He wanted to see his family and friends so he could share their victory with the people that supported them and made their victory possible. As he spoke, there were some of his teammates waving in the background. They were not being interviewed, but it was very clear to everyone watching, they were on the winning team too and were now homeward bound!

Like the little league team from South Chicago, there comes a time when victory is best shared at the home front. As believers in Christ Jesus, one of the most important things that we should always remember is that this place is not our home. Yes, we experience great moments in time, but our real home is to be with God.

Read Philippians 3:20

Paul uses the word "conversation" in verse 20. It comes from the Greek root that means to be a citizen of another country. By this, he meant that he was a citizen of heaven. Are you a citizen of heaven? How can you be for sure? If not, why not become a citizen right now?

Right now in America, immigration reform is the issue of the day. There are millions of people who are in this country, but are not citizens. This means that they have green cards, but no birth certificates. Speaking of birth certificates, do you have one? Not for the United States, but the country of heaven?

Have you ever noticed that you cannot ever be completely happy here on earth? You may be content, but true happiness is always something to be sought. The reason for this is that this is not where you belong. You belong with God. What does this mean to you?

Paul makes it clear that the body that we are in right now will not be able to go home like they are. **Read Rev. 21**. What thoughts rushed through your heart as you read it?

Daily Prayer:

Lord Jesus, this place is not where I belong, and I know it. Like the thirsty deer pants to get to the cool running waters of the brook, so it is that my soul is thirsty for you. I have been calling your name since I was a child, and there are days that I want to put a name with a face. Until that day comes, keep me strong, alert, aware, astute and willing to serve you at all cost for my life's desire is to meet you and hear you say, "Servant, well done!" In Jesus' name, Amen!

Your Journal
Prayers, Thoughts & Notes:

Day 5

A Change Is Gonna Come!

From soccer fields in Germany to cricket fields in Europe; from ice hockey stations in Canada; from boxing rings in Vegas; to waxed wood basketball floors in America; from the grass infields of Tokyo; to the rugged tracks of the Indy 5000, one truth holds solid for every great athlete, time brings about a change. The names fans shouted in 1948 were not the same names they shout in 2014. Champions rise and then fade like the setting of the sun. Men and women appear on the stage of life only for a season and when that season is over, like an actor leaving the stage because his part in the show is over, they simply fade away. Of course, some names will never be forgotten, but for the most part, new names will surface, and it will mark the end of an era and the beginning of a new one.

Much like that of the sports scene, time for the people of God also brings about a change. The change is not radical, but it happens nonetheless. Hair that was black turns white, skin that was once smooth starts to wrinkle, energy that was plenteous now has to be preserved and rest that was once shunned is now a necessity. Time brings about a change.

Paul expresses this unavoidable change to the church in Philippi.

Read Philippians 3:21

Paul talks about the changing of his physical body that he uses on earth to another body that will be used when he reaches glory. Glory will be an awesome place! It will be something that we will never forget.

There's an old cliché that says "everybody wants to go to heaven, but nobody wants to die." In many ways, it holds true. Leaving this place is not something many of us talk about often yet it is a subject of superior necessity. Imagine for a moment that yesterday was your last day on earth. With this in mind ponder the following:

- Where would your soul rest?
- Who would get your house, car, cash, and other things?
- If you have kids, whose custody would they be placed into?
- What would be some of your final wishes?
- If you could write your loved ones one final time, what would you say to them?

The best way for you to live is knowing that one day you will leave. Trips always go smoother when you plan for them ahead of time. You will oneday journey to meet God so plan for that trip too.

Read 1 Corinthians 15:51-58

<u>**Daily Prayer:**</u>

Eternal God our Father, thank you for making room in your Kingdom for a person like me. Your mercy meets my needs; your grace erases my faults; and your blood washes away all of my sins. I know and realize that one day I will meet you face to face. And when that comes I will remember to only give you the glory for what you have done for me. In the meantime, help me Lord, get my life in order so that I live each day like I am preparing to leave so that I can meet you. In Jesus' precious name! Amen!

Your Journal
<u>**Prayers, Thoughts & Notes:**</u>

WEEK 6

IT'S CRUNCH TIME!

Therefore, my brethren dearly beloved and longed for, my joy and crown, so stand fast in the Lord, my dearly beloved. I beseech Euodias, and beseech Syntyche, that they be of the same mind in the Lord. And I intreat thee also, true yokefellow, help those women which laboured with me in the gospel, with Clement also, and with other my fellow labourers, whose names are in the book of life. Rejoice in the Lord alway: and again I say, Rejoice (Phil. 4:1-4).

From its onset, professional basketball like most sports was male dominated.But, on April 24, 1996, the National Basketball Association's Board of Governors made a decision that changed the game forever. The WNBA was born! It gave birth to teams like the Connecticut Sun, Seattle Storm, Tulsa Shock, Chicago Sky, and the Los Angeles Sparks. However, there was one team born out of due season found in the boomtown of Houston that would soon set the stage for what a champion should look like. In the spring of 1997, the Houston Comets were born and these women could play the game with excellence.

Names like Cynthia Cooper, the sister who could run the point; Sheryl Swoopes, the diva with the sweet jump shot; and Tina Thompson, the girl with the game, dominated every opponent who came their way. In fact, these women along with their teammates became the first WNBA dynasty to exist: winning the WNBA Championship in 1997, sending the New York Liberty home to rethink their game strategy, repeating it again in 1998 against the Mercury from Phoenix, and winning back-to-back titles against the Liberty from New York in 1999 and 2000. The Comets were simply awesome. They were women of skill, passion, resilience, and determination. But, that's not what led to the make-up of their dynasty. ESPN news anchor Stuart Scott slam-dunked it when he said, "The difference between the Comets and the other women on the floor was that they were the best in the business at crunch time!"

Crunch time? What's that? When you look carefully at the game of basketball, it is bound by the parameters of time. From start to finish, the game involves time. There is game time, half-time, practice time, time-out, three seconds in the lane which means that you were in the paint with the ball and spent too much time and suffered a penalty, but what on earth was Scott talking about when he mentioned crunch time? Referees can call time-out to discuss a call; a coach can ask for time and get either a 20-second time-out or a full time-out to discuss their next play; at the end of a close game if neither team is winning and the game is in a tie, you can go into overtime; and at the end of the game when the winner has emerged victorious, and the game clock is setting on all zeros it signals that the game is over, and that's game time. But crunch time, what on earth is that?

Players on the court with sweat dripping from their bodies like water from a faucet define it like this. Crunch time is when the whole game has been played, and you find yourself between a rock and a hard place. It is when you can see the hard work behind you and victory is right in front of you, and all you need to do is tough it out. It's the time when you know that what you do next will determine how you end up. Handle your business, and you go home a winner. Mess it up, and you leave a loser. Crunch time happens when your body is tired, you're mentally exhausted, you muscles are aching, the crowd is screaming, the game that was simple is now perplexing and yet the next play requires all that you have in you to pull a victory out of the grasp of a loss. In the eyes of real athletes, game time means almost nothing, that's for the fans. But crunch time is the time when winners become champions and champions become dynasties, and dynasties become legacies!

Crunch time for the Christian is where you end up trapped between worry and trust, panic and prayer, hate and forgiveness, faith and fear, doubt and dependence. Crunch time happens when you are torn between the doctor's report and the Lord's report, what the world is doing and what the Lord is commanding, what they are saying and what the Bible is teaching, what the world is saying is safe and God's Word is calling sin. Crunch time happens when you are trying to grow in the faith but your flesh is pulling you backwards, when your heart is saying that I love God, but your mind is torn between what you want and what God wants for you. Crunch time is decision-making time. Will you speak well of those who have spoken evil of you or will you speak evil of them in return? Will you trust God when life makes no sense or will you walk away from the faith and close your Bible? Will you keep on fighting onward when the Lord moves a loved one from the ranks of your family that you thought belonged to you? Will you trust the Lord when all is failing and collapsing all around you?

Crunch time is not just game time it is prime time! It is that moment when a mature believer in the faith looks toward heaven and declares, "For Christ I live and for Christ I will die."

The Apostle Paul was a crunch time specialist. As he writes the letter to the Philippians, he is in a Neronian prison facing execution. It was crunch time. He is bold in the faith, he is trusting in the Lord and his heart is filled with a joy that only Jesus Christ could give! So that we might learn how to change the game from the life of Paul, let's study what we as believers must do in moments of crunch time that will empower us to become victorious every time.

Week Six

THE GROUP ENCOUNTER

Let's Get Started

1. This is your last group session for this lesson series! You've made it to group session 6. Take a moment and share with your group what this study and their presence has meant to you over the last few weeks. Whisper a prayer thanking God for your time together.
2. Crunch time is real for every believer. Discuss at least one crunch time moment that changed your life forever? What decision did you have to make?
3. Why do you think that God allows moments of crunch time to happen in the lives of Christians?
4. We do not make the best choices all of the time. Discuss at least one moment that you failed at crunch time, but God gave you one more chance.

A Look At The Playbook

Watch DVD for "Group Encounter 6" and complete the section below.

You Must _____ In Perseverance.

If you are going to change the game, you have to be in _____ so that when the game is on the line you can persevere.

Paul admonishes the church to stand fast. It is the word "stay-ko" in the Greek, and it means to Keep on, _____ on no matter what.

Keep this in mind, winners _____ quit and quitters can never _____.

You Must Minimize The _____ and Utilize What You _____.

Confusion often hinders _____ so do your best to rid it.

There were two women and a man mentioned in the passage that Paul used when it was crunch time: Eudia, whose name means safe _____; Synche whose name means fortune _____ and Syzugus, a man whose name means yokefellow or unity _____.

Paul called for them to be of the same _____.

Never forget this, God will never give you what you _____ until you use what you have.

You Must Maximize Your _____.

In 4:4 Paul says, "Rejoice in the Lord alway and again I say _____!"

The term used for rejoice comes from the Greek word "chareo". It means to be_____ in spite of the circumstances.

The _____ of a believer is to rejoice.

When you are in crunch time, the Lord in heaven is in _____ time.

The Locker Room Chat

Take a moment to dialogue and discuss as a group the video

presentation using the questions below to lead the conversation. .

1. Crunch time can be prime time for God in a Christian's life. Often, the Lord works through people to bless you. In what ways have you seen the Lord lift you through the lives of other believers when you were in a crunch time crisis?
2. Have you ever sought to lift another believer when they were struggling or going through a season of lost? What did you do for them and why did you do it? Do you think it made a difference in their lives? Why or why not? Discuss your encounters and thoughts.
3. Christians should live their lives as if every believer in Jesus Christ is a brother or sister in the faith. With this in mind, what could you do as a follower of Jesus Christ that could help others along the way who are living in a crunch right now?

It's Game Time

Prayer Assignment: This week's prayer assignment is a "just do it" assignment. Take a moment to think of someone or some group that is facing a crunch time moment in life right now and encourage them. You may send them a card, call them and exhort them in the faith or do something for them that is a faith project. Whatever the case, within the next seven days, your task is for God to use your life to help someone who is in a crunch to press their way to victory.

Daily Prayer: Lord Jesus, empower me to bless others who are facing moments of hardship. Make my joy full so that my rejoicing causes others to rejoice. God, I realize that the victory that I possess is because I have made a decision to serve you for the rest of my life. Let the service that I do this week bring a smile upon your face as I seek to encourage, exhort, and empower others who are in the midst of crunch time. Lord, I know what you can do when times are tough because you were there for me when life was falling apart. Thank you Jesus, for taking my broken pieces and making me a masterpiece; now I pray, help me to do the same for others. In the name of Jesus, Amen!

Reading Assignment: Read St. John 13:34-35
Memory Verse: Phil. 4:4-Rejoice in the Lord always and again I say rejoice.

Week Six

Day 1

The Danger Of Stress!

It's April 2012, and the soccer team from Britain is on the field. The game is midstream when all of a sudden Fabrice Muamba collapses without warning. Medics and trainers rush to his aid only to discover that he is suffering from cardiac arrest. He is not obese; his blood pressure is great; his glucose is solid; and his cholesterol is 131, perfect. Thank God they were able to revive Muamba, and he's now back on his feet and playing the game that he loves. At only 23 years of age, what was the cause of his cardiac problem?   After doctors had completed an entire physical on Fabrice, they could only conclude that stress was the culprit.

Ryan Shay was not as fortunate. On November 3, 2007, Ryan was in mile five of his Olympic marathon trials. He was rushed to Lenox Hill Hospital in New York where he later passed away. He had just received a clean bill of health from his doctor. He was as healthy as he could be. He was in great physical shape; his diet was fabulous; and he had the physical anatomy of a runner. What caused his heart problem? Here is the answer, the very same thing that caused Muamba's heart problem, stress.

Let's be honest, there are times when family issues, financial woes, pressure to produce, jealous co-workers, problems at home, issues with colleagues and just plain ole anxiety can cause more problems in your life than what meets the eye. Stress is a killer, but the Lord of heaven has given believers a way to handle it before it damages you.

Read Philippians 4:5-7

Stress can come from numerous sources. Take a moment and list the three top things that cause you worry, anxiety and stress from time to time.

1. _____
2. _____
3. _____

In the passage, Paul tells the Philippian Church to "….be careful for nothing"; a better translation of this phrase would be worded like this, "don't let your troubles, trouble you." Do you think it is possible for you to have trouble, but your trouble not bother you at all? Be honest in your answer. _____Yes _____No

Here's a moment to rejoice for you! There is a way for your stress to never stress you out again. Paul gives the formula and format for stress-free living in verse 6.

- First of all, he says Pray (Take your worries to God and leave them there).
- Secondly, he adds with Supplication (Be specific about what you need).
- Lastly, Paul commands Thanksgiving (Boast on the grace of God).

Paul says that when we do our part, the peace of God protects our minds and hearts. In what ways do you need God's peace right now?

Here's how you attain and retain God's peace, let go of it and let God have all of it today!

Read Proverbs 3:5-7

<u>**Daily Prayer:**</u>

Lord, there are times in my life when I am completely stressed out worrying about things that I cannot change. Forgive me for not trusting you enough to leave my worries completely with you. God, from this moment forward, I am making a choice never to worry again. Instead of worrying, I choose to live knowing that you will always take care of me and any situation that comes my way. I celebrate your grace right now because you have proven to be an all- sufficient God and a wonderful Master. I love you, and I praise you for blessing me with a worry free life. In the name of Jesus Christ, Amen!

Your Journal
Prayers, Thoughts & Notes:

Day 2

Both Rags and Riches!

The Golden Triangle of Texas is a small composite of three cities. Beaumont, Port Arthur and Orange, respectively makeup the Triangle. Within this small cluster of cities comes a host of athletes who have been blessed to play as professionals in the sports that they love.Great athletes like:

- Bubba Smith
- Kendrick Perkins
- Jerry LeVias
- Warren Wells
- Christian Michael
- Jerry Ball
- Frank Middleton
- Gus Holloman
- Taylor "Tank" Reed
- Stephen Jackson
- Anthony Guillory
- Tody Smith
- Omar Sneed
- Jesse Phillips
- Dwight Harrison
- Bob Pollard
- Kenna Young
- Bobby Pollard
- Billy Wright
- Wayne McDerman

And the list goes on. Though their sports may be different, the one thing that is common amongst them is the fact that many of the athletes are from very meager beginnings. In fact, it is commonplace to hear the rags to riches stories of these greats. They know the hurt and pain of poverty, and yet they are blessed to enjoy the financial bliss of economic solvency.

Paul too knew and understood what it was like to have more than what he needed and how to survive with leftovers that he had to make stretch.

Read Philippians 4:8-13

Do you know what the pain of poverty feels like? If so, take a moment to reminisce. What was it like for you?

When you look back over your life do you have more now than you've ever had before? Why do you think God has favored your life in such a way?

Paul says, "I can do all things through Christ, who strengthens me." What do you think he means by this statement? How does it apply directly to you?

Read 1 Peter 5:10

In what ways has the God of all grace blessed you? Be specific.

Daily Prayer:

Eternal God my Father, I know what it feels like to just barely have enough and I know what it is like to have more than what I really need. In both instances Lord, I have learned how to trust and depend on Jesus Christ. Lord, you have been so good to me, and I realize right now that I can do anything if you are with me! Thank you Jesus for never leaving my side, for always being there for me and for blessing me the way that you have. I love you, and I will praise you for the rest of my days. In Jesus' name, Amen!

Your Journal
Prayers, Thoughts & Notes:

Day 3

Real Friends Show Up When Things Are Down!

It is impossible to tell who your real friends are when everything in life is great. However, when the chips are down, things are not well and affliction finds your address, that's when things become very clear. It is what took place in the life of sixteen-year-old Salisbury High School student Shaleek Williams. It was an accident that could have ended his life as he suffered a gunshot wound as a high school student. Shaleek is a super athlete at his school. He got caught trying to break up a fight when one young man pulled a gun and fired a shot. When people started to scatter, Williams fell to the ground. A stray bullet had hit him.

In the heavy fog of media criticism, lies, and bad information getting to the press, many of Shaleek's so-called friends abandoned him in his time of need, but his teammates showed up in grand fashion. "They were there for me," Williams said. And as soon as he could walk again, Shaleek Williams pressed his way into the gym to support his teammates in a game at his school. When asked what he learned from this experience, young 16-year-old Shaleek Williams replied, "The choice to try and break up a fight nearly cost me my life. I will never do that again. And, now I know who my real friends are. Real friends show up for you when things are down."

The church at Philippi was not just a group of people that Paul preached to. They were a group that would show up for the Apostle when things were down.

Read Philippians 4:14

Like the Philippian Church was to Paul, every believer needs someone who will show up when life is filled with affliction. Look back over your life. Who was there for you?

In many cases, the people that you have helped are sometimes not there to help you. Why do you think this is the case?

Make a short list of people who are your true friends.
- _____
- _____
- _____

What is it that makes these people very special to you?

Normally, the people who come near us in times of trial and affliction remind us of Jesus Christ. How do the people on your list remind you of the Lord? What characteristics do they possess that make you say, "They remind me of Jesus Christ"?

Read Psalms 27:10

Daily Prayer:

Lord Jesus, thank you for the people that you have placed in my life who are my real friends. I lift them before you right now in a measure of prayerful intercession, and I ask that you bless them, strengthen them and keep them in your mighty hand. God, my friends, are precious to me because they remind me of you. Jesus, you are the best friend that I have ever had in my life! You know all that there is to know about me, and you love me still. I bless you this day, and I thank you for all that you mean to me. In Jesus' name, Amen!

Your Journal
Prayers, Thoughts & Notes:

Day 4

Give And It Shall Be Given!

What do Lebron James, Derek Jeter, Serena Williams, Clayton Kershaw, Larry Fitzgerald, Eli Manning, Albert Pujols, David Beckham, and Tiger Woods all have in common? It is not race, age, sexual gender or sport. It is the fact that they are the top ten givers among professional sports athletes in America. These super athletes know and understand the one true principle of life and living that makes this world a better place to live. They know that you make a living by considering what you make, but you make a life by giving to the less fortunate so that they might have an opportunity to make it.

Dwayne Wade, however, has taken his giving to a level of faith and obedience. He gives ten percent of his earnings to his church as taught in the scriptures. He believes in his heart that if you give to God, He will always give to you.

Read Philippians 4:15-19

It is possible to give without loving, but it is impossible to love without giving. To say you love God makes you prove that love through your giving as a Christian. Examine your giving for a moment. Are you a tither? Why or why not?

Have you ever experienced God where you gave to help others, and the Lord turned and opened a door for you that blessed you in return? What happened?

Givers are always gainers. The more we give, the more we gain. What are some things that you could give more of knowing that it would please God if you gave it? Be specific.

When Paul declares that "....my God shall supply all of your need according to His riches and glory by Christ Jesus," he is speaking only to those who have blessed him as a Pastor. Just like you would leave a grace gift (gratuity/tip) on the table for a waiter, you should leave a gift for your Pastor. What type of gift do you normally leave for your man of God? Be honest. How much was the last tip you left a waiter at a restaurant after you paid the bill? Did you leave the waiter that filled your tea glass more than you left your Pastor who feeds your soul? Food for thought, just like you tip a waiter for blessing you while your flesh eats, bless your Pastor for making sure your faith eats.

Read St. Luke 6:38, St. Matthew 6:19-21

What do you see in this verse that you can apply to your everyday life?

Daily Prayer:

God, all of my life you have given to me in one way, or another. Your greatest gift you've ever given to me was your only-begotten Son Jesus Christ. Lord, everything that I have you have given it to me, and I feel compelled to give more to you. So right now, O God, I give you my mind, my heart, my resources, and my life. I submit myself to you so that you can give me away for your glory. Lord let the seeds that I sow in the fertile soil of ministry return to me as you have promised. I love you Lord Jesus, and I praise your name. Amen!

Your Journal
Prayers, Thoughts & Notes:

Day 5

He Keeps The Glory From The Truth Of My Story!

John Blake is a CNN columnist who recently wrote an article entitled "When Did God Become a Sports Fan" in which he took a look at athletes who openly thanked God for their performances. The resolve to Blakes' query is not that God is some grand sports enthusiast seated in heaven cheering His team to victory. However, God is a sovereign and supreme deity who loves all of His creation, but has a special place in His heart for His children. And His children have a special place in their hearts for Him.

When an athlete thanks God for blessing him or her with victory, it is simply an open admission that if it had not been for the Lord on my side this victory would not be happening. In short, it is an athlete's way of saying "God, you keep the glory from the truth of my story!" It is his or her way of saying, "I may be playing the game, but you are determining the outcome!"

Blake asks an interesting question regarding God and the loser in events when athletes don't say much about God. Blake asks, "Where is God in the loser's locker room?" To which the gracious response to such an interrogative would be God is too big to be in just one locker room. He is in both sharing equally. To the winner, He is a fortress and vicar who has pressed them to victory. For the loser, He is a confidant, friend and restorer of hope when all seems lost.

In short, God is simply an awesome God who deserves all of the glory from the heart of every story win, lose or draw!

Read Philippians 4:20-23

Daily Prayer:

Lord, I want the world to know that you are my God because I want the glory from the life you have given me to be yours exclusively. God, I seek to keep none of your glory for myself. I want it all to go to you. Jesus, you keep the glory, just let me tell my story everywhere I go! In the name of Jesus, Amen.

Your Journal
Prayers, Thoughts & Notes:

CPSIA information can be obtained
at www.ICGtesting.com
Printed in the USA
FFOW05n0315071214

9 781597 552851